Beyond US and THEM

How to Communicate Across Political Divides

By

JOANNA MICHAL HOYT

Beyond US and THEM

Copyright © 2018
All rights reserved. This book or any portion thereof may not be reproduced or used in any manner whatsoever without the express written permission of the publisher except for the use of brief quotations in a book review.

ISBN: 9781976970184

Warning and Disclaimer
Every effort has been made to make this book as accurate as possible. However, no warranty or fitness is implied. The information provided is on an "as-is" basis. The author and the publisher shall have no liability or responsibility to any person or entity with respect to any loss or damages that arise from the information in this book.

Publisher Contact
Skinny Bottle Publishing
books@skinnybottle.com

Beyond Us and Them

"I am convinced that men hate each other because they fear each other. They fear each other because they don't know each other, and they don't know each other because they don't communicate with each other." — Martin Luther King, Jr.

"We're in the age of communications more and more, though we're in communication less and less." — Wright Morris

Each day's news reflects the harm caused by our fear and our inability to communicate. Economic and political alliances as well as nations are coming apart, split by growing mistrust. Far-right parties are gaining strength even as their rhetoric grows more extreme; in some places far-left movements are also rising. We're hearing more and more extreme rhetoric from public figures — speech that suggests that their opponents are evil or subhuman. Hate crimes and terrorist incidents are also on the rise, carried out by people who seem to have taken the dehumanizing messages to heart. Inside my own country, the U.S., we are unable to deal even with the obvious problems that all parties agree we have —the drug abuse epidemic, the lack of affordable health care, the overcrowded prisons —because the opposing parties have become so adversarial.

It would be comforting to blame this deepening divide on a few demagogues in high places. But it's not that simple. The unprocessed fear, anger and mistrust of ordinary people is driving us further apart. In a 2016 Pew survey of U.S. voters, about half the members of each major party reported being afraid of the other party. About the same number of voters saw members of the other party as being highly close-minded. Somewhat smaller — but still substantial — groups believed that members of the other party were also dishonest and immoral.[1] Over the past year, my Facebook feed has featured stories in which public figures with a clear political affiliation have been caught speaking offensively or acting dishonestly. The stories and the comments below them go on to say that this horrible behavior shows how disgusting, dishonest, heartless and hypocritical all the people ideologically aligned with the fallen figures are. My liberal friends are making these posts about conservatives and vice versa.

Sometimes, calls for a return to civility are met by a significant objection: Our political differences aren't trivial preferences. They involve serious moral questions and issues of life and death. When the stakes are so high, we can't just relax and make nice. We have to stand up for the people who will be crushed if the wrong policies are approved. After all, if we legitimize our opponents' positions, aren't we emboldening the violent extremists on the fringes of those positions?

The violent extremists seem to have a different view of political polarization. In August 2017 the leader of a small neo-Nazi rally in Arlington, Virginia told reporters, "We're very encouraged generally about the mood of the country ... We think things are moving towards radicalization and polarization. I know a lot of people think polarization is a bad thing, but we don't."[2] History suggests that he has reason for thinking in this way. Dictatorships — both fascist and Communist — have arisen in times of extreme polarization, when people found some other group to blame for all their society's ills and treated those people as less than human. Venezuelan economist Andrés Miguel Rondón described the basic strategy of demagogues this way: "Find a wound common to many, find someone to blame for it, and make up a good story to tell. Mix it all together. Tell the wounded you know how they feel. That you found the bad guys. Label them: the minorities, the politicians, the businessmen. Caricature them. As vermin, evil masterminds, haters and losers ... , you name it. Then paint yourself as the savior. Capture the people's imagination. Forget about policies and plans, just enrapture them with a tale. One that starts with anger and ends in vengeance... Populism is built on the irresistible allure of simplicity. The narcotic of the simple answer to an intractable question." [3]

Terrorism, of course, has a similar narcotic allure. Both neo-Nazis and ISIS enthusiasts have bought into the idea that the people on the "Other Side" are evil; that it's impossible to negotiate with them, and that we simply have to eliminate them. Denouncing all conservatives as fascists, or all Muslims as terrorists, strengthens the extremist narrative. The only way to bring people back from the outer reaches of hate is to reach out to them as human beings; to show them that the people they fear and hate have something in common with them. This may be wearying, frightening, thankless work, but it has been known to succeed. I will share some success stories later in this book.

Even outside dictatorships and hate groups, polarization and alienation make it harder for us to confront the real and difficult questions of our days. Most of our intractable questions require complex solutions. In order to deal constructively with the challenges posed by the unprecedented migration of refugees from disaster areas, or with the crises triggered by climate change, or with rising debts and rising wealth gaps, we will need to think in a way that is detailed, complex and unspectacular. We'll need to balance values and concerns that urge us in different directions. It's hard to do that well in the heat of a shouting match.

In order to solve our problems, we'll also need the strength and resilience that come from trust in our neighbors and in ourselves. Polarization makes true democracy practically unworkable. It undermines the trust on which democracy is built. It isolates us from our neighbors. It leaves us lonely and afraid. Social researcher Brené Brown writes, "The world feels high lonesome and heartbroken to me right now. We've sorted ourselves into factions based on our politics and ideology. We've turned away from one another and toward blame and rage. We're lonely and untethered. And scared. So damn scared."[4] This is a miserable condition to be in. And it's not a condition from which we can meaningfully advance any of the causes that we hold dear.

If we truly care about the well-being of our neighbors, our nations and our world, we need to learn to communicate with each other. We need to stop shouting our talking points and start actually listening. We don't have to disown our convictions or deny our disagreements, but we have to listen with open minds. We may find some common ground from which to work for political solutions. Even if we can't reach agreement on policy specifics, this kind of brave and civil conversation restores trust and connection, and it destroys the fear and loathing which demagogues can so easily use to divide us. That was Rondón's strongest prescription for working against dictatorship and preserving a free society: Let people know each other as neighbors, not as enemies.

It's easy to say that we need to communicate. It's much harder to figure out how to do that well at a time when simplistic arguments and extreme partisanship are so common. It's hard because our differing convictions are rooted, not only in differently conceived ethical foundations and disparate news sources, but also in in powerful personal experiences of pain and love, and in the fierce desire to belong to a group. Nevertheless, it needs to be done.

This book doesn't offer a failsafe guide to constructive dialogue. I don't believe such a thing exists. It does offer some suggestions for learning to understand our own motives as well as the motives of folks who disagree with us, some techniques for holding conversations that don't devolve into shouting matches, and some resources for further reading and practice.

Where I'm Coming From

I'm not writing as an objective observer. I come to this book with my own fervent convictions. Sometimes it's hard for me to take my own advice and try to understand the people who disagree with me on key issues rather than dismissing them as cruel or stupid.

I'm fortunate in having grown up among friends with opposing views. When I was a child, my family belonged to two homeschool groups. One was a rural group of Christian homeschoolers, mostly conservative; the other was an urban-centered group of unschoolers of various faiths, mostly liberal. My family was the only one to belong to both groups. There were kids I felt close to and adults I admired in both. The first group could sometimes be heard deploring the immoral and irresponsible ways of Democrats; the second deploring the cruel and senseless ways of Republicans. In both cases I thought, "But I know some of those people, and they're not really like that ..."

As an adult, I am somewhat able to "pass" as liberal or conservative, and I have things in common with friends on both sides. I'm a committed Christian, a homeschooler, a farmer, a celibate teetotaler living and working alongside a parent, and a faith-based volunteer. On that basis, I fit in well with many conservatives. I'm a Quaker interested in interfaith dialogue, an unschooler and an organic farmer working at a nonprofit. On that basis, I fit in well with many liberals. When it comes to politics, I fall on the liberal side of many issues (pacifism, support for immigrants and refugees, concern about systemic racism, passion for economic reform, belief in marriage equality, concern about climate change, etc.), and on the conservative side of a few (opposing the legalization of drugs, and supporting more leeway for homeschooling and other forms of alternative education when it's not conducted for profit.) I also know, love and respect people who disagree deeply with me on every one of these issues. In my country's ongoing bitter debate over abortion, I see a deep moral dilemma that may be impossible to legislate in a way that truly protects the rights of the woman and the child. Most of the people I know find this position weak and untenable, though they disagree about which side I should come down on.

I value my friendships and challenging conversations with people who disagree with me. But I've found these harder to sustain over the past year and a half. Some of my friends have become louder and angrier and made it clear that they don't want to hear from people who disagree with them. Some have become quieter and say that there's no point trying to talk about anything political because it all turns so ugly. I want to keep the conversations going and to keep them friendly, but sometimes I forget my good intentions. I lash out when my sore spots are prodded and I have to apologize afterward. I hold my tongue because I want to avoid conflict or to be liked; later on, I unpleasantly surprise the other person by stating my real convictions. Messy as the process is, I remain convinced that we need to stay in dialogue. This book is the record not of my brilliant successes, but of a few things I've learned in the course of trying.

Part I: The Great Divides

Chapter 1

Moral Foundations

"When we listen to a political leader, we don't simply hear words; we listen predisposed to want to feel certain things ... Some feel proud of a 'Give me your tired, your poor, your huddled masses' Statue of Liberty America, while others yearn to feel proud of a Constitution-abiding, work-your-own-way-up America." — Arlie Russell Hochschild, *Strangers in Their Own Land*

This Bridge Will Only Take You Halfway There

It's easy to say that we need to find common ground. It's harder to identify just where that shared starting place is. Sometimes I think I've found a shared value to build on, and then I realize I'm wrong. My conversation partner and I have been saying the same words but meaning different things by them; we still aren't reaching each other at all. In those moments, I remember a poem by Shel Silverstein which begins "This bridge will only take you halfway there ..." The illustration shows a walker who has climbed the graceful curve of a very high bridge only to find that it breaks off abruptly at the peak. The figure is gazing wistfully down at a city built on a distant hill, quite visible and quite inaccessible.[5]

A shared faith tradition doesn't always provide political common ground, though we can easily assume that it should. My friend, "L," recalls an occasion when she was out with a conservative friend. A friend of that friend who didn't know L, came up to them in a state of obvious excitement, started to talk, checked herself, pointed to L and asked their mutual friend, "Is she a Christian?" Answered in the affirmative, she laughed with relief and said, "Oh, Good. So we're all Republicans here ..."

It's true that at this point in the U.S., Republicans are much more likely to be churchgoers. But this is a relatively recent phenomenon, and religion still drives passionate politicking across the political spectrum.

Jim Wallis and Franklin Graham, both committed evangelical Christians, are profoundly convinced that the Bible lays out a clear ethical vision with obvious political implications. But they disagree completely on what those implications are. Both have Bible verses and ardent followers to back them. Some Christians cite the Biblical narratives of holy war and argue that military victory is a sign of God's favor; others cite Jesus' refusal to let his followers defend him with deadly force, and argue that war is a clear violation of God's commands. Some Christians cite the Apostle Paul's injunction to submit to the governing authorities and say that civil disobedience is ungodly; others point out that Paul, like Jesus, was executed by the governing authorities and say that civil disobedience is clearly part of the prophetic tradition. When food assistance to low-income families is being discussed, the Bible is again invoked on both sides. I've seen other Christians invoking Paul's injunction in 2 Thessalonians 3 that "the one who does not work shall not eat." This generally prompts me to say something about the difficulty of finding work, and the fact that much necessary work is not paid or not paid adequately. I tend to counter-quote Matthew 25, where Jesus tells people that he is welcoming them into his kingdom because they fed him when he was hungry, clothed him when he was naked, visited him when he was sick and in prison, etc. The people to whom he speaks say that they never met him, and Jesus tells them that what they have done for the least of his brothers and sisters is what they've done to him. Christians who disagree with me sometimes say that the point of this passage is that charity gets you into heaven, and that being taxed on behalf of the poor isn't charity and doesn't get you into heaven. I say the point is not afterlife insurance; the point is that every person is a God-bearer, every human being matters and deserves access to the essentials of life ... and the argument spins out from there.

Many conservatives and many liberals agree that we need civil discourse, but we define civility differently. I recently became aware of this in the course of a long-running and fairly friendly exchange with a friend who runs a small conservative blog where I have occasionally published guest posts from the other side. His comment policy and his mission statement called for civil discourse. He and I both understood this to mean no name-calling, no obscenities, and no appeals to violence. Beyond that, our understandings diverged.

I thought civility meant not making sweeping negative statements about groups (Christians are bigots/Muslims are terrorists/The Other Party's followers are hypocritical, dishonest, cruel ...) I believe such statements are false. I believe good and evil are present in all races, religions and parties. I also think such statements destroy the basis for constructive conversation, which I understand to be humility, open-mindedness and recognition of our common humanity. But I came to realize that some conservative friends see what I call civility as stifling political correctness. They say it denies the truth — some really believe (for instance) that Islam promotes terrorism or that Democrats are godless socialists and that they have the right to say so. If they can't say those things, they feel they can't meaningfully participate in the conversation.

I was startled when my conservative friend said that civility includes showing deference to the flag, the national anthem and other national symbols, and speaking of America as the best and greatest country in the world. He believes that America is self-evidently better than all other countries and that criticizing America destroys the basis of constructive political conversation. For him, that basis is a shared loyalty to and celebration of America. I see this as stifling blind loyalty. I think that the U.S. is a nation like the rest, with many things to be proud of and many things to be ashamed of. I think that America does not in fact offer 'liberty and justice for all' within its borders and that it has also acted to destroy life, liberty and justice outside its borders. If I am not allowed to say that, I can't meaningfully participate in the conversation.

These shared words that mean different things. These bridges that don't connect can be intensely frustrating. It's tempting to dismiss them by assuming that the people who understand key words and values differently are ignorant or hypocritical. But when I actually take time to listen closely to where the folks who disagree with me are coming from, I generally find honest conviction and significant thought behind their words.

Once we admit that thoughtful and decent people may interpret the values we cherish in ways that we find incomprehensible or even repellent, we're left with the long slow work of trudging back down off our hanging bridges, examining the ground again and trying to understand the depth, extent and origin of the divides between us. This can be a slow and disheartening process. But I believe that we can only find true unity once we understand the depth of our differences.

That search for understanding requires us to let go of our own preconceptions and listen deeply and openly to our unlike-minded neighbors. Before we can let go of our own preconceptions, we have to see what they are and come to some understanding of how we formed them and why we hold onto them.

The different understandings of liberals and conservatives are shaped in part by different news sources and echo chambers, which I'll address in later chapters. They're also shaped by the fact that we frame morality very differently. Psychology professor Jonathan Haidt's 2012 book, *The Righteous Mind: Why Good People Are Divided by Politics and Religion,* tried to map those different frames. Haidt began as a liberal trying to understand what motivated conservatives; his research moved him into a position somewhere between the usual ideological groups. He spent a long time posing wide-ranging ethical questions to people of different cultures, religions and political groups and then trying to understand how they reached their answers. He began to find consistent patterns in the answers given by people of different political persuasions.

Haidt identified six different "moral foundations" upon which we base our decisions: *Care/harm prevention, fairness, loyalty, authority, purity/sanctity,* and *freedom.* He found that liberals and conservatives tend to prioritize these foundations in very different ways — and also that they tend to define them differently.

The *care/harm* foundation is the basic urge to protect and nurture vulnerable creatures. Haidt argues that this is hard-wired into us, perhaps as a result of the evolutionary importance of caring for and protecting our children. When we see someone being hurt, the "mirror neurons" in our brains fire as though we had been hurt ourselves, and we naturally want to stop that hurting. Experiments suggest that this instinctive compassion has some limits. Subjects may not react as strongly to the pain of someone who belongs to a distrusted out-group, or to the pain of somebody whom they've seen acting in a way they disapprove of. But principle may pick up where instinct leaves off, prompting us to try to protect others from harm even when we don't identify with or approve of them. The experience of our own faults and loneliness may also prompt a more visceral identification with others who have misbehaved or who are ostracized.

Haidt says that both sides value care and the prevention of harm. However, care is one of the two primary foundations of most liberals, whereas conservatives see it as one of many important values to be balanced.

Conservatives are also more likely to set tighter boundaries on their compassion, and on the group of people for whom they care deeply. Haidt writes that, for conservatives, compassion "is not universalist; it is more local, and blended with loyalty."[6] I have seen these different boundaries in play in the immigration debate over how we admit refugees and asylum seekers. Liberals point out the desperate situations which refugees are fleeing and say that there's a clear humanitarian imperative to offer these refugees a safe haven. Liberals are particularly apt to tell stories of children endangered and seeking safety, and to believe that any decent person would understand that it's wrong to leave a child in danger of starving or being killed. Conservatives often say that admitting refugees endangers their fellow citizens. Sometimes this danger is described in terms of crime or terrorism, sometimes in terms of overloading social safety nets or overcrowding spaces. Some appear to believe that any decent person would care first and foremost for the children who are already their fellow citizens. Anti-immigration advocate Peter Brimelow made the foundation of this belief visible to me in his book, *Alien Nation*, where he quotes Proudhon as saying, "If all the world is my brother, then I have no brother," and goes on to decry what he calls 'promiscuous altruism'."[7]

This disagreement is pragmatic as well as moral. I see refugees making positive contributions and I figure that it's more dangerous to wall people out and leave them crowded in refugee camps which may incubate diseases or a degree of hopelessness which may lead to terrorism. In the end, it is our different takes on the essential moral value of compassion that fuel the emotional intensity of the immigration debate.

The *fairness/cheating* foundation seems as though it should be intuitively obvious: Everyone should get their share and what they deserve; no one should take advantage of anyone else. The rub is that we calculate deserving in different ways. Haidt wrote, "Everyone cares about fairness, but there are two major kinds. On the left, fairness often implies equality, but on the right, it means proportionality — people should be rewarded in proportion to what they contribute, even if that guarantees unequal outcomes." I've heard the different meanings of fairness in play as my friends on opposite sides of the political spectrum discuss tax policy. To my liberal friends, fairness obviously means that everyone gets their basic needs met, and it's fine if that involves some curtailment of wealthier people's discretionary spending. To my conservative friends, fairness obviously means that people who worked hard and earned money shouldn't have it taken away from them and spent on people who haven't worked as hard. (The assumption that hard work reliably generates large amounts of money, and that the possession of large amounts of money reliably indicates hard work, seems doubtful to me and to some of my fellow liberals, but that's another story.)

Both sides in the American political debate express outrage at the unfairness of our political and economic system. The ire of the Left tends to be focused on very wealthy individuals who are seen as living in luxury while others go without necessities, and using their power to warp the economic and legal system to ensure that no one challenges their advantages. The ire of the Right tends to be focused on welfare recipients whom they describe as free riders, non-workers appropriating to themselves the fruits of others' labor, and also on the politicians whom they see as using welfare money to buy the votes of those non-workers, thereby ensuring the continuing success of the politicians.

Furthermore, *fairness* is the other moral foundation (along with *care*) which liberals tend to see as absolutely essential, while conservatives see it as one of many important values to be balanced.

The *loyalty/betrayal* foundation refers to identifying strongly with your group —your family, your nation, your religion, your party — and protecting its members, its reputation and its interests. Loyalty may require and motivate great personal sacrifices. It may also make the loyalist more willing to do harm to members of out-groups in order to protect the loyalist's own group.

Conservatives tend to place a high value on loyalty and to emphasize the self-sacrifice which it requires. Some aspects of this become obvious in public debates: Conservative leaders are much more apt to emphasize nationalism/patriotism, reverence for the flag, and loyal adherence to the tenets of the conservative's religion (though this may not inspire respect for those who adhere loyally to the tenets of a different religion.) It also appears in the daily lives of conservatives. Study after study reports that conservatives are more likely than liberals to stay long-term in the same neighborhood, the same church and the same job. They're also more likely to live in close-knit, homogeneous rural communities.

Liberals are more likely to be concerned with the shadow side of loyalty — the willingness to sacrifice the well-being of some other group to the well-being of our own group. Liberal leaders are more likely to talk about diversity, open-mindedness and egalitarianism. Liberal individuals tend to be more mobile; traveling readily between places, jobs and congregations. They are also more likely to live in large, loose-knit, heterogeneous cities.[8]

However, both liberals and conservatives show a strong tendency to cluster with people who share their political persuasions, to stand up for them, to sacrifice some of their own beliefs for the sake of group unity, and to verbally attack members of the other group who are perceived as threatening their group. There'll be more about that in Chapter 4.

The *authority/subversion* foundation prioritizes maintaining an orderly hierarchy. Usually in an authority system, each person has clear responsibilities to the people both above and below them in the chain. Deference and obedience are owed to people higher up, care and protection to people lower down.

In many cases *authority* is prized more highly by conservatives than by liberals. Linguist George Lakoff said American society was divided between the "strict father" and the "nurturant parent" models of family life. In the 1990s and 2000s, researchers asked voters whether it was more important for children to: Show independence or respect for elders, obedience or self-reliance, curiosity or good manners, consideration or good behavior. They also asked which candidates the voters intended to support. Those who emphasized respect for elders, obedience, good manners and good behavior overwhelmingly expressed their intention of voting for Republicans. Those who emphasized independence, self-reliance, curiosity and consideration overwhelmingly said they'd vote for Democrats.[9] Haidt said that liberals are more likely to view authority as synonymous with oppression.

However, there's a catch here. In many situations, liberals are more likely than conservatives to defer to academic experts. This becomes particularly evident in the ongoing political debate over human contributions to climate change. Liberals repeatedly point out the overwhelming consensus of scientists and peer-reviewed studies that the burning of fossil fuels is a major driver of climate change. Conservatives repeatedly indicate their distrust for experts. A 2016 study showed that liberals were much more likely than conservatives to trust the authority of university scientists and science museums (though no more likely to trust the authority of industry scientists, and far less likely to believe that religious leaders could make authoritative pronouncements on questions of science.)[10]

The *sanctity/degradation* foundation rests on our instinctive responses of reverence and disgust. In cognitive form, it is the sense of an intrinsic, natural or divinely sanctioned order which should not be violated, even when violations wouldn't be obviously wrong according to any of the other moral foundations. Respectful treatment of dead bodies is one example of a nearly universal, strongly held value that rests almost exclusively on this foundation.

Haidt says that conservatives tend to value *sanctity* much more highly than liberals do. Certainly, the public conversation around sexual ethics seems to reflect this. Liberals are much more apt to frame the ethical questions around sex in terms of consent, freedom and the avoidance of harm, and conservatives to speak of what is natural and Godly as opposed to what is degraded. But liberals have their own sanctity/natural order issues. Joan Dye Gussow, who studies and writes about issues related to global food production, lamented the rapid spread of pollen from genetically engineered corn in the U.S. and the possibility that soon there will be no remaining corn seed that hasn't been altered by cross-contamination. "This is a fist in the eye of God," she said, "and I'm not even all that religious." [11]

Haidt's original classification system ended there, positing that liberals primarily valued care and fairness, while conservatives equally valued all five foundations. Later research prompted him to add another foundation, *liberty/oppression* — concern for *freedom* from bullies and tyrants.

Like fairness, *liberty* is highly valued on both sides of the aisle, but people mean different things by it. Americans across the political spectrum are likely to say that we value freedom., We also go on to say that our preferred party is obviously defending freedom against the aggressive encroachments of the other party. Most of us find our side's monopoly on freedom to be self-evident. Clearly, we are using the word to mean different things.

Conservatives and libertarians tend to talk about the freedom of individuals and businesses from government regulation and redistribution. Liberals tend to talk about freedom from social conditions that restrict people's lives and liberties — discrimination, poverty, etc. They often believe that government can have a helpful role in preserving this kind of freedom. Haidt also says that liberals are more likely to be concerned about protecting the freedoms of underdogs anywhere and everywhere (thus tying back into *Care* and their understanding of *Fairness*.) Conservatives were particularly concerned with protecting the freedom of their own groups — religious, political, or geographical — against outsiders (thus tying back into *Loyalty*.)

Arlie Russell Hochschild, a very progressive Californian who decided to go reside with and listen to very conservative Tea Party members in Louisiana, said "I hear a lot of talk about freedom in the sense of *freedom to* — to talk on your cellphone as you drive a car, to pick up a drive-in daiquiri with a straw on the side or to walk about with a loaded gun. But there was almost no talk about *freedom from* such things as gun violence, car accidents, or toxic pollution." She went on to quote a Louisiana resident who was pushing, against a strong tide of public opinion, for tighter environmental regulation: "People think they're free when they're not. A company may be free to pollute, but then people aren't free to swim."[12]

Libertarians would put the issue in different terms. Instead of freedom to pollute, they might speak of freedom to innovate and take the necessary risks which enable economic growth and technological progress. Hochschild also quotes a Tea Party enthusiast saying, "You want everything to be perfect, for the companies to make no mistakes, and you — and we — can't live like that „, We have to be able to take risks. That's how they split the atom— risk." [13] (Many of Hochschild's hosts also argued that existing rules weren't actually very effective at protecting against violence, accidents and pollution, and they thought stricter rules would inhibit freedom without doing much for safety.)

Haidt has made his research available online, and continues to ask people to take online surveys to help him refine his vision further, at www.yourmorals.org . This research is being conducted internationally, and the liberal/conservative divides he describes seem to resonate in many cultures.

There is another basic divide in moral conceptions which Haidt does not address, which may be peculiarly American. Certainly, the U.S. has been the epicenter of the Prosperity Gospel and its sibling, *The Power of Positive Thinking.*

American minister and author Norman Vincent Peale taught that our thoughts shape reality and that we can attain our goals by thinking positively. "Stamp indelibly on your mind a mental picture of yourself as succeeding," he told followers. "Hold this picture tenaciously. Never permit it to fade."[14] "When you expect the best, you release a magnetic force in your mind which, by a law of attraction, tends to bring the best to you." He's often described as an influence on the subset of evangelical Christianity which is often called the Prosperity Gospel. In this Gospel, health, wealth and success are described as blessings given by God to those who show their trust in God's goodness by believing and acting on the belief that they will be given everything they want and need.

This affirmation-based thinking has gained prominence among conservatives with the rise of Donald Trump. Peale praised Trump before Trump entered politics. Trump has praised Peale and described himself as "a firm believer in the power of being positive,"[15] and Trump's statements about himself, his supporters and the nation he now leads (although not about people he disagrees with) are full of relentless affirmations: The greatest, the best, the biggest, unprecedented, winning ... This language seems to resonate with many of his supporters. Hochschild wrote of her Tea Party hosts, (many of whom were struggling financially), "What seemed like a problem to liberals — the fact that conservatives identified 'up,' with the 1 percent, the planter class, — was actually a source of pride to the Tea Party people I came to know. It showed you were optimistic, hopeful;, a trier... That gaze forward, even when matters seemed hopeless, was a feature of the brave deep-story self."[16] For people with this worldview, ambition and affirmation, together with reluctance to apologize, second-guess oneself or look back at the people being left behind by success, appear as moral virtues.

To many of Trump's liberal critics, this extreme form of positive thinking appears as a moral and practical fault. Identification with the wealthiest is seen as likely to promote lack of compassion for the poor, who, according to the liberal view, are poor not because of their moral failings or bad attitudes but because of a rigged social system. Refusal to apologize is seen as arrogance. Refusal to acknowledge problems looks like recklessly courting disaster. Humility, willingness to admit fault, and adherence to the precautionary principle are all seen as virtuous qualities.

This liberal/conservative split on positive thinking presents a striking contrast with another widely identified psychological difference between liberals and conservatives: Conservatives tend to be more fearful and more primed for threats. Studies have measured this in several ways. The brain's amygdala, which handles emotional processing and threat responses, tends to be larger in self-identified conservatives than in self-identified liberals. Conservatives were more likely than liberals to focus on and respond strongly to disturbing/threatening images instead of pleasant/relaxing images in the same computer-generated collages.[17] Other studies have found that randomly selected subjects who have just been exposed to frightening or disturbing stimuli give more typically conservative responses to political questions than randomly selected subjects who have just been exposed to reassuring stimuli.[18]

One group of studies addressed both sides of this odd dichotomy. The researchers found that conservatives reported greater happiness and satisfaction with life than liberals. On the other hand, analyses of photos and speech transcripts from conservative and liberal politicians showed the liberals were more likely to use positive language, to smile, and to smile with their eyes as well as their mouths. Photo analysis for ordinary voters (self-described liberals and conservatives on LinkedIn), showed the same pattern. The lead researcher was hesitant to explain this discrepancy, but made this suggestion: "It's not that conservatives are lying about their happiness. They just have a more confident style of self-assessment where they evaluate themselves positively across a whole bunch of different kinds of traits, and happiness just appears to be one of them."[19] Others have suggested that the higher levels of fear in conservatives make them more determined to bravely focus on the positive, or to desperately deny the dangers they can't bear to face — depending on one's perspective. This argument makes some sense to me. I value honesty and courage very highly because neither of them comes naturally to me. I sometimes go out of my way to admit mistakes in cases that others see as unimportant, precisely because I am trying not to slide into the easy habit of lying. Positive thinking could conceivably be a similar counterbalance against fear.

On the individual and practical level, there seem to be advantages and drawbacks to being overly confident/positive. Optimism and avoidance of thinking about negative possibilities can increase people's odds of surviving and recovering from serious illnesses; but it can also make them more likely to smoke, have unprotected sex or otherwise seriously risk their health.[20] It can motivate people to achieve feats that are difficult but not impossible, or it can prompt them to exhaust themselves taking on impossible tasks. Where is the balance point? That's a difficult question, and finding the answer becomes even more difficult when we overreact to the other side's actions.

The positive thinking/realistic thinking divide may be connected to another virtue which liberals and conservatives agree on praising and disagree on defining. That is courage. Hochschild reflected on a conversation she heard between two friends while visiting and listening in Louisiana. Donny, who did factory work involving high exposure to dangerous chemicals, supported the deregulation of factories. Mike, working in a safer job, put a great deal of energy into trying to hold companies accountable for the pollution which was very evident in local soil, air and water. She wrote that the two men "assigned honor differently... Exposed to danger in some of his jobs, Donny tended to stand brave against it and to value bravery. ... Donny said, in essence, 'I'm strong. Mother Nature is strong. We can take it...' [Mike] valued the precautionary principle and said, in essence, 'The real strength we need is to stand up to industry and the almighty dollar.'"[21] Hochschild often described the value her Tea Party hosts placed on not complaining, not asking for help, and not grieving too much over losses seen as inevitable. One woman told her, "I think a lot of activists are self-serving. You have to put up with things the way they are. Pollution is the sacrifice we make for capitalism."[22] And, as she noted, "Word from the Lake Charles pulpits seemed to focus more on a person's *moral strength to endure* than on the will to change the circumstances that called on that strength."[23] More liberal Christians (those I'm most apt to read and listen to) emphasize the will and the courage to stand up and change unjust circumstances. They invoke the faithful resistance to the dominant system embodied by Moses, the Old Testament prophets and Jesus, and urge present-day Christians to follow their example.

When I listen to my own friends on different ends of the political spectrum, I often hear this divided concept of bravery. My friend the conservative blogger, and some of his like-minded guests, have argued that the highest degree of courage and virtue is shown by the citizen soldier who unquestioningly risks his life for his group and in obedience to his superiors. I see the courage this would require. I see the harm that such soldiers suffer and I believe that they deserve the best care and support we can give them. However, I am more likely to admire the courage of conscientious objectors who stood up against heated public opinion and legal punishment because they weren't willing to harm others. I notice that my conservative friends are more apt to speak admiringly of courage manifested in enduring danger, loss and hardship without asking for help or sympathy, and my liberal friends to speak admiringly of courage manifested in challenging the systems that create danger, loss and hardship. (Sometimes, both sides dismiss the others contemptuously as cowardly whiners and slackers, or as cowardly mindless sheeple.)

I suspect that if we discussed specific situations deeply and thoughtfully, most liberals would value willingness to endure life's suffering, and most conservatives would value willingness to stand up against injustice. The Serenity Prayer, beloved by many on both sides of the aisle, speaks of the need to change what can be changed and accept what cannot be changed. Perhaps we don't agree about what changes are possible. Perhaps if we could stop overreacting to each other's positions, we'd be better able to have that conversation.

Chapter 2

Stories

"And truth is this to me, and that to thee ..." – Tennyson, Idylls of the King: The Coming of Arthur

Still a Man Hears What He Wants to Hear...

Liberals and conservatives increasingly differ not only on what we think should happen, but also on what we think is actually happening now. Is human activity changing the climate? Are black Americans more likely than white Americans to be killed by the police? Has the Affordable Care Act increased or decreased health care costs? Is immigration increasing or decreasing the U.S. crime rate? Are Christians being systematically discriminated against by U.S. law, or using U.S. law to systematically discriminate against other people? Most of my friends have emphatic and unequivocal answers to all these questions, answers which fall consistently along party lines. This could indicate a deep desire to conform to their groups (which we'll talk more about in Chapter 4.) It could also reflect the fact that they're getting their news from different sources.

The news media is notoriously polarized and fragmented. This is somewhat true of the television news networks which many Americans rely on. FOX viewers and MSNBC viewers will get very different news stories and very different commentary. I tend to see PBS, the BBC and the CBC as providing fairly balanced coverage, but my more conservative friends say that these are left-leaning. Bias is determined in relationship to a center of accurate information, and there's less and less clear consensus about where that center lies. We may agree that *The Wall Street Journal* is somewhere to the right of *The Washington Post*, but that's far from bringing us to agreement about which of them is slanted and which is objective.

The political differences between reputable news sources are obviously expressed in their opinion pieces, and in the emotional weight of the language they use in their news stories. Stronger leanings are also expressed in the stories they choose to cover. There are some major headline events which all sources cover, but beyond that, there's a lot of room for editorial discretion. Conservative sources may have more to say about scandals affecting liberals, and liberal sources about scandals affecting conservatives. Conservative sources are more likely to tell stories about welfare fraud and voter fraud (especially if the latter is committed by liberals or minorities), and liberal sources are more likely to tell stories about people being denied clearly needed benefits and about voter suppression. In this way, liberals and conservatives who stick to their preferred outlets for news can inhabit very different political realities — even if their preferred sources don't actually run fake news stories.

The Internet and social media offer a wider range of news and "news sources" and a greater divide in what's shown as real. *The Wall Street Journal* offers a webpage called Blue Feed, Red Feed (http://graphics.wsj.com/blue-feed-red-feed/) which shows Facebook posts from both sides of the aisle on various topics. They choose stories which have received a large number of views and come from widely followed sources. Sources which are frequently shared by people with a broad range of self-identified political leanings don't appear in the feed; stories from sources frequently shared by people who fall on only one side are shown on that side's feed. What I see there reflects what I see on my own Facebook feed, since my relatives and friends tend to be politically opinionated and also to hold opposing opinions. Today under

"Health Care," Blue Feed runs stories about the termination of a program funding medical insurance for children which Red Feed ignores, but both sides are mostly occupied with President Trump's actions to weaken the Affordable Care Act. Blue Feed explains that this will deny vital health care to millions of Americans and cause prohibitive expenses for more and that this is motivated by greed, hardheartedness, and a blind will to demolish President Obama's legacy. Red Feed explains that this is an urgently needed attempt to undo the previous President's tyrannical practices which allowed the government to bankrupt taxpayers and force them to buy unwanted health care at inflated prices and that opposition to President Trump is fueled by greed and blind will to preserve President Obama's legacy. The stories on both sides seethe with moral indignation. Under "Guns," Blue Feed appeals to non-gun owners who fear being killed by irresponsible gun owners, and Red Feed to gun owners who fear being tyrannized and perhaps killed by irresponsible liberal government agents.

Both sides also have some 'news sources' which run fake stories, clickbait with overly drastic titles, and quotes and incidents wrenched out of context to inspire outrage. Where do they come from? We often don't know. Recent Congressional testimony has shown that as many as 126 million Facebook users in the U.S. may have seen political content generated by Russian fake accounts during the 2016 election.[24] This content didn't just push particular political candidates; it also deliberately played up tensions between members of different races and religions in the U.S.[25] This appears to be a fairly effective way of destabilizing American politics and culture. But while a hostile government may have exacerbated our polarized discourse, it didn't create it. There's plenty of extreme content coming from native-born Americans across the political spectrum. And, whatever their sources, rumors are only effective when people choose to pass them on and believe them — or at least act as if they're true.

We're reluctant to look closely at the accuracy of stories and headlines that resonate emotionally with us. The most dramatic example I've encountered (on Facebook, but not on the WSJ's Red Feed column) was a piece titled "Pro Baseball Stadium on Lockdown After THOUSANDS of Screaming Muslims Swarm the Field for SICK Reason."[26] The text of the article showed that what actually happened was that a Muslim group reserved the baseball field one day for an Eid celebration which was attended by thousands. Those who entered had to pass through a metal detector because there was concern about anti-Muslim violence. Nevertheless, the comments below the article seemed to reflect the title more than the actual content. When I tried asking some commenters what they were upset about, their answers suggested that the very existence of Muslims in the U.S. scared and offended them, and that even if there hadn't actually been a Muslim attack on a baseball field yet — there surely would be someday.

Recently, some of my liberal friends posted a meme claiming that Vice President Pence said that poor people needed faith in Jesus Christ, not health insurance. What followed was furious commentary on the disgusting heartlessness of Republican Christians who just want the poor to die. Some of my other liberal friends fact-checked this and pointed out that the quote was fake — Pence hadn't actually said it. The original posters agreed that the quote might be faked, but some went on to say that it hardly mattered since he was a despicable man who probably thought things like that even if they didn't say them out loud. The comment threads continued with enthusiastic denunciations of Pence and his ilk.

It seems that the emphatic assertion of something that fits our preconceived fears strikes us as convincing whether or not we find the facts behind the assertion convincing. The Stanford experiments of the 1970s showed that this tendency exists even outside the fractious realm of politics. In one experiment, students were asked to distinguish between real and fictitious suicide notes. Some of them were told they had chosen correctly in nearly all cases, others that they had almost always been wrong. Then the students were told that the test results they had received were fake and that the researchers were simply trying to gauge their responses to thinking they were right or wrong. Then the researchers asked them how well they thought they had actually done. Those who had been told they were almost always right — and then told that that the previous statement was faked —still believed they were above average. The students who had been told they were almost always wrong — and then told that the previous statement was fake — still believed they were below average.[27]

Another problem is that there's very little agreement these days about how to verify information. Which news sources are credible? Which fact checking sites are credible? Which scientific studies can be trusted? Given the amount of information coming at us each day and our lack of ability to fact-check directly, this is bound to be a fraught and complex question. We tend to solve it simply, though not usefully, by believing the evidence which supports our existing opinions. In another Stanford experiment, students were asked their views on capital punishment as a deterrent to crime. Then they were shown two studies, one supporting and one refuting the deterrence claim. Both studies were made up, and carefully designed by researchers to use equivalently weighted evidence. Then students were asked if their reading had changed their views on capital punishment. All of them came away more confident in their existing opinions.[28]

This confirmation bias is exacerbated by the echo-chamber effect. The political posts of friends on my Facebook wall are typically followed by a long string of agreements and amplifications in the comment section. Occasionally there will be a dissenting voice —sometimes careful and polite, sometimes loud and furious — but mostly I see social media being used to amplify agreement. When there is disagreement, it's more likely to be a fine-point (though still sometimes impassioned) disagreement between two people who share a party affiliation, such as a Clinton Democrat disagreeing with a Sanders Democrat. Sociologists Dale Miller and Deborah Prentice noted that, "When members of the same group discovered they disagreed about something, the instinct was to come together, to talk about their differences. Friendship within the group might be strained by the dispute, but at least there was usually discussion. When the disagreement occurred between members of different groups, however, the typical reaction was avoidance and silence."[29] That is, there was silence between groups, but a louder and louder buzzing of conversation within each group about the awful thing Those People Over There just said ...

This echo-chamber effect begins with human choice. Today it's exacerbated by the computer algorithms that track our preferences as we participate in social media or browse the Internet. Techno-sociologist Zeynep Tufekci describes how these algorithms, initially designed to promote consumer goods to receptive buyers, also target people with political content that amplifies their current ideas and emotions. When Tufekci repeatedly watched a YouTube video of a Trump rally in order to analyze it,

YouTube began showing white supremacist videos in her sidebar. When she watched one of these, her sidebar filled with more extreme and graphic hate content. Tufekci tried repeatedly watching Hillary Clinton videos on YouTube and watched her sidebar fill with increasingly bizarre left-wing conspiracy theories. She didn't think this was the result of deliberate political manipulation by the creators of YouTube's algorithms. She noted that moving people to more extreme content is likely to keep them engaged with the site longer, which means they will look at more ads. Whatever the purpose may be, the effect is pernicious: Online, we are pursued by content that amplifies our existing prejudices, and we are less and less likely to see content that might challenge our current point of view.[30]

It's not only published news sources that divide us. What we hear in person is also likely to confirm our existing opinions. That's because we're extremely and increasingly likely to do most of our listening to People Like Us. This is not altogether a new problem. Women have long been more likely to talk to other women than to men about their experiences of sexual assault or harassment; men have been more likely to talk to other men than to women about times when they felt they were falsely accused of sexual harassment. This has sometimes resulted in the different genders having strikingly different narratives and failing to understand each other. But over the past 50 years, the gaps have widened as the U.S. has increasingly sorted itself into communities of politically like-minded people. As Bill Bishop observes in *The Big Sort*, "we now live in a giant feedback loop, hearing our own thoughts about what's right and wrong bounced back to us by the television shows we watch, the newspapers and books we read, the blogs we visit online, the sermons we hear, and the neighborhoods we live in."[31]

Americans have become less tightly tied to the neighborhoods where they're born, to their religious denominations, and to fraternal organizations which used to bring people from different parties together. We have begun to sort ourselves geographically, with liberals moving to majority-liberal communities and conservatives moving to majority-conservative communities. In 1976, one-quarter of American counties went for one presidential candidate or another in a landslide victory. In 2004, that figure had risen to one-half.[32] Over the same time period, churches became less politically diverse — both because Christianity and conservatism became more tightly aligned and because liberal and conservative Christians increasingly sorted themselves into different churches. Participation in fraternal organizations bottomed out. To an ever-greater extent, Americans are living, worshipping, and often also working with, people who shared their own opinions and fears. I have read that the same sorting is taking place across Europe, but I don't have the academic or cultural knowledge to trace the timeline or the scope of this process. Chapter 4 looks more closely at the wide-ranging effects of this division.

Lies, Damn Lies, and ...

"Those who can make you believe absurdities can make you commit atrocities."
— Voltaire

Our fragmented views of reality may play out in either one of two equally dangerous ways: We may wholeheartedly believe that the stories which support our preconceptions are self-evidently true and the stories which don't fit our preconceptions are self-evidently false. This way of thinking encourages us to take increasingly extreme political positions, and also to become increasingly suspicious of those people who disagree with us, whom we may see as lying about self-evident facts.

Or, bombarded by claims and counter-claims of fake news, we may give up on the very idea of verifiable truth. This may be even more dangerous. In 1951, Hannah Arendt wrote in *The Origins of Totalitarianism,* "Mass propaganda discovered that its audience was ready at all times to believe the worst, no matter how absurd, and did not particularly object to being deceived because it held every statement to be a lie anyhow. The totalitarian mass leaders based their propaganda on the correct psychological assumption that, under such conditions, one could make people believe the most fantastic statements one day, and trust that if the next day they were given irrefutable proof of their falsehood, they would take refuge in cynicism; instead of deserting the leaders who had lied to them, they would protest that they had known all along the statement was a lie and would admire the leaders for their superior tactical cleverness ... The ideal subject of totalitarian rule is not the convinced Nazi or the convinced Communist, but people for whom the distinction between fact and fiction (*i.e.,* the reality of experience) and the distinction between true and false (*i.e.,* the standards of thought) no longer exist."[33]

Brené Brown, writing in 2017, quoted Harry Frankfurt's definition of bullshit: "Someone who lies and someone who speaks the truth are playing on opposite sides, so to speak, in the same game. Each responds to the facts as he understands them ... The bullshitter ignores these demands altogether. He does not reject the authority of the truth, as the liar does, and oppose himself to it. He pays no attention to it at all. By virtue of this, bullshit is a greater enemy of the truth than lies are."[34] She notes that bullshitting plays a major role in our politics today — in speeches made by political leaders, in slanted news coverage and also in our own daily conversations. This can be a cynically used technique. It can also be an unhelpful but quite understandable human response, based, in Brown's view, on two basic wishes. One is the wish to appear informed; always to be ready with an opinion and not to "lose ground" by admitting you don't know something. The deeper wish is to advance a cause seen as morally important. Brown describes it this way: "Our intentions may not be to manipulate, but to force the point that we're in a situation where neutrality is dangerous. I actually agree with this point. One of my live-by quotes is from Elie Wiesel. 'We must always take sides. Neutrality helps the oppressor, never the victim. Silence encourages the tormentor, never the tormented.' The problem is that the emotional plea is often not based in facts, and preys on our fears of not belonging or being seen as wrong or part of the problem. We need to question how the sides are defined. *Are these really the only two options?*"[35]

This isn't to deny that politics confronts us with urgent moral choices. But the choices are often more complex and less extreme than our polarized discourse makes them appear. We'll look more closely at the roots of this problem in Chapter 4.

Honest Fiction

Our conceptual frameworks and our emotional responses are shaped not only by news, real or fake, but also by the up-front fictional stories we consume. Italian professor Loris Vezzali studied the effect of one particularly popular set of stories on the attitudes of children and teenagers toward members of stigmatized groups. First his researchers asked Italian elementary students about their attitudes toward immigrants. Then they divided them into two groups: One of which read prejudice-related passages from the Harry Potter books, while the others read neutral passages. Then the researchers asked the children about their attitudes toward immigrants again. The groups who'd read about Harry's friends being stigmatized for their ancestry had a much more positive view of immigrants after those readings than before. The other students hadn't changed their views over the same time period. Later studies showed that Italian high school students reported more positive attitudes toward gay and lesbian people after reading the Potter books, and that English university students showed more compassion for refugees after reading them.[36] This effect was apparently taken seriously by white supremacists who recently gathered for a second mini-rally in Charlottesville, Virginia and chanted not only "Blood and Soil," "The South will rise again," and "You won't replace us," but also "Harry Potter is not real!"[37] The most ardent Potter fans would hardly quibble with that statement, taken literally. But apparently identifying with — or being appalled by — fictional characters primes our emotional responses to real-life situations that remind us of the stories we've read, inspiring us to act like our imaginary heroes (or to avoid acting like their antagonists.)

I'm not aware of research on an anti-Potter (a fictional work that tends to reduce people's sympathy for out-groups in general.) But I do know that fiction can prime people's attitudes on both sides of some particular issues.

A 2003 study found that people who watched crime shows regularly were more afraid of becoming the victims of crime and tended to have more punitive attitudes toward justice (emphasizing the punitive role of the law, supporting the death penalty and longer sentences, etc.) Researchers thought this might be because crime shows tend to feature violent and random crimes and to end with the guilty person being arrested. The study's authors noted that TV didn't make a big difference in the views of people who had significant direct experience with crime or with law enforcement, but did seem to affect people who didn't have such firsthand experience. These viewers know that they're watching fictional shows, but the shows still give them a set of images, a story about how the world and the law operate that feels true.[38] And these felt attitudes may influence their perception of suspects or inmates in general, even when they know consciously that the real-life circumstances aren't the same as those in the shows.

I've experienced the feels-true effect in my own attitude toward criminal justice, which was shaped by a different set of fictional stories. I was 10 or 11 when my mother and I saw a film version of Victor Hugo's *Les Misérables*, with its sympathetic depictions of desperate people who weren't able to get what they legitimately needed while staying within the law, and who were punished excessively once they broke the law. The story stuck in my mind. I read the book and spent a lot of time brooding over it, imagining myself in various of its scenes, and wondering what it would take to make the society of the book — or my own society — into a place where people weren't pushed into committing crimes and/or where they were helped — not just punished — after committing them. Later, when I heard reports of jailbreaks, my instinctive sympathy was with the escapees, even if in fact, they'd been convicted of violent crimes in what appeared to be fair trials.

Recently, when my state senator raised vehement objections to a state plan to expand education for prisoners, I called and wrote her to express my own support for inmate education. I made the practical argument that education has repeatedly been shown to reduce recidivism. I believed that, but I was also thinking indignantly, "These people need and deserve to be helped, not just punished!" In reading the senator's Facebook page I realized that many of my fellow constituents felt strongly that prisoners were vicious and deserved stringent punishment. I found that hard to understand. I checked my own mind for instant associations with *prisoner*. I came up with a bunch of names. Some came from news stories and history books: Nelson Mandela, Daniel Berrigan, Dorothy Day, and other political prisoners I admired; Kalief Browder, incarcerated for years awaiting trial for a very minor crime of which he was never convicted, eventually committing suicide, etc. But many of my associations came from novels: Jean Valjean, Sirius

Black, Frodo Baggins, Harriet Vane from *Strong Poison*, Tom Robinson from *To Kill a Mockingbird*, Anatole from The *Poisonwood Bible* ... Once again, my list was a combination of brave people imprisoned for standing up to oppression and innocent people wrongfully convicted; most of them were badly treated in prison. I surmised that my fellow constituents on the other side must have been hearing very different stories about prisoners, and I daydreamed about getting more people to read *Les Misérables*.

And then I found that Donald Trump, who favored a very tough approach to criminal justice and a very hands-off approach to social justice, had used a clip from the musical version of *Les Mis* at a campaign event. I was shocked — more so, oddly, than I was by the fact that Trump enthusiasts sometimes quoted the Bible.

Plainly, then, we can read the same stories and derive completely different lessons from them. Why is that? What is it in our minds that sets us up to respond so differently?

Chapter 3

The Heart Has Its Reasons...

"The heart has its reasons of which reason knows nothing." –Blaise Pascal

Before we can talk effectively to other people, we must learn to listen to them. Before we can meet them where they are, we need to understand where they're coming from. It may also help us to look more closely at the emotional roots of our own convictions, to understand why we hold them so passionately and perhaps to notice our own sore spots and blind spots.

Most of us can supply long lists of apparently rational arguments for our moral positions, but conviction generally does not begin at the rational level. Much of the passion we bring to ethical disagreements comes from our own deeply felt experiences of love, loathing, fear and trust; experiences which are evoked by news stories and political arguments in ways that may be complex and surprising. We'll examine that in this chapter. Some of that passion also comes from our fervent wish to *belong*, to be part of a group of people bound by a common story and a common sense of purpose. We'll look at that more closely in Chapter 4.

The emotion underlying our moral decisions is often decried by disputants who mock "muh feels" arguments and claim that policy should be determined in accordance with pure reason. (Those who say this often go on to say, generally without citing evidence, that their side of any given political debate is clearly making evidence-based rational arguments while the other side is whipping up emotions and making no sense. Some go on to suggest that intelligent people are chiefly members of their own party.) But this claim has a fundamental flaw: If we were capable of pure logic untainted by emotion, that logic alone could not tell us what we *should* do. It could lay out the likely consequences of any particular action ... but something beyond reason is required to tell us which consequences are preferable. Man does not live by reason alone. So political disputes do need to rest on a clear perception of verifiable facts. But in order to determine our response to these facts, we have to turn to the more subjective realm of ethics.

Our moral reasoning is based on emotion and intuition at least as much as reason. Jonathan Haidt, who identified the different moral foundations discussed in Chapter 1, cites brain scan research showing the immediate and intense activation of emotional centers in the brains of subjects presented with moral dilemmas, and the strong correlation between the depth of subjects' emotional reactions and the decisions which subjects made after their reasoning functions had time to work. Haidt also argues that moral reasoning's main function seems to be to justify what we already feel to be right. He cites a study by reasoning researcher David Perkins which gathered information about participant IQ and then asked participants to consider thorny social questions, state their own opinions, and then write down all the relevant arguments for and against that position which they could think of. Participants with higher IQs typically generated more arguments for their own positions ... but their intelligence didn't help them to generate more arguments on the other side. Perkins concluded that "people invest their IQ in buttressing their own case rather than in exploring the entire issue more fully and evenhandedly."[39] Remember this next time you're appalled to find an obviously intelligent person subscribing to an opinion which you find unjustifiable.

The final problem is practical and relational. When people express a passionate political opinion, there's a good chance that they're speaking from the pain of traumas in their own lives or in the lives of people they love. Until that pain is heard and acknowledged, they're not going to be very able to step back and consider counterpoints rationally.

I've certainly experienced this in my own life. When I am feeling extremely angry, defensive, ashamed, or distressed, I find it much harder to think clearly about the specific problems that have caused my distress and the specific steps I need to take to address them. I have to acknowledge and deal with my emotions first; then, with a bit of detachment, I can think clearly and calmly about specifics. Throwing syllogisms and statistics at someone in distress is not a practical strategy. Furthermore, if the other person is lumping you in with other people who have hurt them or their loved ones, they're probably not going to trust you, listen carefully to you or give you the benefit of the doubt.

This doesn't mean that we should just go with our emotions. We don't always think clearly about the experiences that move us. We may distort our responses by overgeneralizing or by denying what we think we can't bear to know. We cannot and should not get rid of the emotional components of our decision-making, or that of other people, but we can and should look clearly at them and see whether clarification and healing are possible.

In this chapter, we'll look at some of the ways in which our experiences shape the moral intuitions which drive our moral reasoning. Thinking more carefully about this may help you to understand the seemingly inexplicable positions your opponents take. It may also help you to understand your own.

Trauma, Pain and Compassion

"I imagine one of the reasons people cling to their hates so stubbornly is because they sense, once hate is gone, they will be forced to deal with pain." — James Baldwin

Sometimes our political views are shaped by our own painful experiences, or those of the people we love. These come in several forms.

The most obvious are cases in which we or our loved ones have been directly hurt by other people we can clearly see and identify. We may respond to pain by broadly distrusting and resenting people who share some demographic characteristic with the person who hurt us. Real traumatic experiences can easily lead to false overgeneralizations about Those People.

Sometimes this happens when we have a bad experience with someone from a group we don't normally interact with. I know people who are suspicious of interracial marriage because someone they loved married someone of another race and the marriage broke up in a storm of vitriol. Most of these people also know some people in same-race marriages that turned toxic, but they know enough people in healthy same-race marriages so that they don't generalize.

If the pain is great enough, exposure to a large number of people from the target group may not help. I'm Christian. Once when I spoke at a spiritual conference I heard from some people who were angry with me for using what they considered excessively Christian language. My first unhelpful impulse was to feel persecuted and to blame the objectors for being narrow-minded. Instead, I thought a bit about it and asked if they could tell me why they were upset. They could and did. One person who took offense at my remarks was Jewish and had been harassed by some of my fellow Christians because of her faith. Her experience of harassment was made more painful and daunting by the family memories of pogroms that had been passed down to her. Another person whom I'd offended was gay and had been disowned by Christian family members who told him he was a pervert bound for hell. When they listened to my faith language, they heard echoes of the people who had tormented them.

I also support marriage equality, and I was disturbed when a Christian acquaintance began to talk about "homosexuals" as dangerous perverts. I thought of some of the gay and lesbian folks I love and admire — and of the gay man mentioned above — and I took offense. I also took a deep breath, said that hadn't been my experience of the gay and lesbian folks I knew, and asked what had led to her opinion. She told me. A man had sexually abused a boy in her family who later committed suicide. His relatives found out about the abuse in the boy's suicide note. When she heard anything about gay men, she thought of the man she held responsible for that boy's death.

I do not believe that most Christians are bigots, or that most gay and lesbian people are sexually abusive. But before I could say that, I needed to acknowledge the very real pain underlying the views that had troubled me. I was talking to people who had suffered terribly, and who had drawn sweeping conclusions based on that pain.

To each of them I said something inadequate along the lines of, "That is terrible. I am so sorry that you had to endure that." I listened a little more. Once the other people felt that had been heard, I was also able to speak in a way they could hear. I told the Jewish woman that I was a Christian grateful to Judaism for the foundation of my own scriptures, and for Jesus, and also for the writings of Elie Wiesel, Chaim Potok, Howard Kushner and Martin Buber, and the deep well of spiritual strength that sustained some Jews I knew and admired. I told the gay man that I was a Christian who believed that gay and lesbian people and their unions were created and blessed by God. I told the Christian woman that I had worked with and grieved over girls who'd been sexually abused by men, and that I knew and loved gay and lesbian couples whose faithfulness and goodness to the people around them were admirable. That said, I thought child abuse and sexual orientation were not linked to each other.

At that point, the other people seemed able to hear me. The people at the conference weren't about to become Christian, nor did I wish they would. But I hoped they might not assume hate the next time they heard Christian language. The woman at the church meeting wasn't going to start supporting marriage equality, but I hoped she might be a little less likely to assume that gay and lesbian folks were predatory and that their supporters didn't care about children. I hadn't changed their minds, but I hoped I had softened the polarization a little.

If we've been hurt by a variety of people, it seems psychologically easier for us to put all our blame and anger on the ones who least resemble us. In his book, *The Autobiography of a Recovering Skinhead,* Frank Meeink describes growing up with a variety of parental figures (white, as was he) who were addicted and abusive. Some of them beat him severely. Meeink went to a largely white elementary school for many years and got into quite a few brutal fights with his classmates. Then he moved to a predominantly black school where he was sometimes beaten up for being a white kid.

Meeink felt wretched about himself. Then he met some white supremacists who explained to him that black people just were naturally violent and hated whites. That the violence and the drugs disseminated by black people had corrupted white people, so they couldn't even love their own families properly. That explanation consoled Meeink. He could tell himself that the abuse he had suffered wasn't his fault, and it wasn't the fault of his parents, it was the fault of people like the black schoolmates who hit him — people whom he did not resemble, love or need. He could tell himself that he was part of a powerful movement to destroy the evil in the world by attacking black people, gay people and others who threatened his righteous kind.

Meeink broke free of these stereotypes the hard way. He ended up in prison after a racist attack. Some of his fellow prisoners were also white supremacists. Some of his fellow prisoners were black. When his girlfriend broke up with him, it was a black man who offered him sympathy and understanding and some hope, while his white fellow inmates laughed at him for expecting her to do anything other than cheat on him. Back out of prison, and back with white supremacists, Meeink began wincing at racist jokes, remembering the man who had comforted him. Then he began hearing some of his supremacists buddies mocking Italians — and Meeink was partly Italian. He backed out of those groups slowly. Then the Oklahoma City bombing happened, and Meeink saw people who looked like him grieving for their loved ones killed by a man who'd thought some of the same things Meeink thought. He understood the harm he had done by misreading the causes of his pain. He was appalled, and after that he poured his energy and fervor into helping other people get out of hate groups. [40]

People who have been traumatized are not doomed to a life of prejudice. Social researcher Brené Brown writes that there are three ways to deal with pain: "You live in constant pain and seek relief by numbing it and/or inflicting it on others; you deny your pain, and your denial ensures that you pass it on to those around you and down to your children; or you find the courage to own the pain and develop a level of empathy and compassion for yourself and others that allows you to spot hurt in the world in a unique way."[41] Our world is the richer for the courage of people who have owned their pain and let it move them to deeper awareness and generosity.

Some adults who were abused as children come away from that experience with a burning determination to protect disempowered people from abuse by authorities. Sometimes this expresses itself in laboring to protect other children in troubled homes; sometimes it's turned toward other situations, such as protecting civilians in their own country against excessive use of force by police, or civilians in other countries from their country's military operations. Some even extend their compassion beyond the human world. Author and environmentalist Derrick Jensen's memoir, *A Language Older than Words,* describes how the violence he witnessed and suffered in his home when he was too small and powerless to protect himself left him deeply sensitized to the suffering of other defenseless creatures destroyed by human greed.

Other forms of trauma can also lead to courage and compassion. South African archbishop Desmond Tutu grew up suffering from the cruel injustices of the apartheid system. He acted heroically in the struggle to overthrow that system and create a society in which black people were treated as fully human. His compassion for suffering people led him to gentleness and concern for the well-being even of the people who had mistreated him and his fellow black South Africans. That experience also sensitized him to the pain and frustration of all manner of groups who suffer from discrimination around the world. He has advocated tirelessly for the rights of other persecuted ethnic minorities, for gay and lesbian people, for unregistered children, and many more.

We grieve for others' sufferings as well as our own, and that grief can feed both compassion for sufferers and anger at those whom we blame for those sufferings. My views on refugee policy are deep and visceral, and I find it hard to listen calmly when people support turning more refugees away, though I am working on this. I've been lucky in never having to flee my home or my country but I have loved people were less lucky.

I had an older friend whose immediate family (who were Jewish) got out of Hungary just ahead of the Nazis when he was 5 years old. His parents told him they were going on a vacation and he couldn't understand why there was so much shouting and crying about the extended family members who couldn't come. As an adult, he became a dedicated peacemaker. He said he had forgotten Hungarian completely, but he cried out in his sleep, and it wasn't in English.

As a teenager, I volunteered at an ESL center on Saturday afternoons, helping to teach a class of Sudanese and Somali kids between 4 and 8 years old. I remember their wide-eyed curiosity about everything new, their overflowing energy, and their bouts of homesickness — and the way they talked matter-of-factly about people who were killed or maimed by land mines. They struggled to wait for food to be passed to them at snack time because they'd spent their formative years in places where there wasn't enough to go around and you had to snatch what you could and eat it fast before someone else grabbed it.

I can and do make statistically-backed arguments about why accepting refugees is good for our national character, our economy, our national security, and the safety and vibrancy of our neighborhoods. I think my reasoning is sound. But my urgency around this issue, and my struggle to converse civilly with people who disagree, comes from my memories of my friend and my students.

I know people who bring this kind of passion to both sides of the abortion debate. Some are parents, siblings or friends of severely disabled kids whom someone had suggested aborting. It pains them deeply that their loved ones were dismissed as unfit to live. Some are parents, siblings or friends of women who were forced to bear children conceived by rape or who got illegal abortions that endangered their lives. It pains them deeply that their loved ones were made to suffer.

Who Did This?

Sometimes it's easy to pinpoint the people responsible for the suffering that shapes our convictions. Sometimes it isn't. In the latter case, people may respond to the same traumas with profoundly different political opinions.

In *Strangers in Their Own Land*, Arlie Russell Hochschild describes living among and listening to workers in a part of Louisiana devastated by pollution. Some of her hosts had been farmers until their cows died of drinking polluted water. Some had lived partly by fishing until the fish were so laced with heavy metals that no one would buy them, and locals were increasingly leery of eating them. Some had lost their homes to sinkholes caused by deep drilling to inject toxic waste; many had loved woods walks and bird watching until the trees and the birds died. Most of her hosts had lost loved ones — often several loved ones — to cancer and respiratory illnesses probably related to their contaminated air and water. They were living in the midst of a disaster that was destroying the place and the community that they loved.

Hochschild was bewildered by the fact that, in the face of this destruction, they supported the Tea Party and its agenda of deregulation. She had expected them to blame the petrochemical companies whose effluent had poisoned their water and air. What she found was that instead, they blamed the regulators who had not prevented, held companies accountable for, or even adequately acknowledged the destruction.

Hochschild's stories made that focus of anger understandable. She described a 2013 explosion at a factory which sent up spectacular clouds. Given the materials the factory worked with, those clouds were likely to carry toxins including hydrochloric acid and vinyl chloride. Drivers on the nearby freeway stopped to photograph the clouds; several of these then had to be rushed to the ER because they couldn't breathe. The freeway was closed and residents were told to shelter in place. "But," Hochschild added, "the Louisiana Department of Environmental Quality reported that its detection equipment showed N.D. — 'non-detect.' Citizens were left to reconcile the fact that their iPhones and computer screens were saying 'plain, obvious, terrible' and the state was saying, 'Didn't see it. Can't tell.'"[42] She quotes one resident saying, "The state always comes down hard on the *little* guy... Take this bayou. If your motorboat leaks a little gas into the water, the warden'll write you up. But if *companies* leak thousands of gallons of it and kill all the life here? The state lets them go. If you shoot an endangered brown pelican, they'll put you in jail. But if a company kills the brown pelican by poisoning the fish he eats? They let it go. I think they *overregulate* the *bottom* because it's *harder* to regulate the *top*."[43] [Emphasis hers.]

In contrast to their understandable anger at regulators, most of Hochschild's hosts seemed curiously willing to accept the behavior of the corporations. There are several possible explanations. Some people thought the companies, at least, were honest actors behaving predictably—they say up-front that they just care about making money, and that's what they're doing. The regulators, on the other hand, are supposed to be protecting people and the environment, but they seem to be either corrupt or asleep at the wheel. Some of Hochschild's hosts expressed admiration for petro company employees who work high-risk jobs and contempt for regulators who are less likely to be blown up or poisoned on the job. Perhaps most importantly, they saw the companies as made up largely of people like themselves and their neighbors, while the government seemed remote and alien. One woman told Hochschild, "Pollution? I don't talk about it much with friends. This whole town operates off of oil. So I could be talking to two moms whose husbands work in the plants. They think government regulations will hurt jobs, or stop new plants from coming in. You don't want to *remind* them of dangers. Or make them think you're *blaming them* for the work they do. It's too close to home."[44]

And that is the other major driver of our felt convictions. What is close to home for us? Who are our people, and what do we feel that we owe them?

Chapter 4

Our People

"Scapegoating reinforces the joyous unity of the gathering. The act of casting out the 'bad one' helps the fans unite in a shared sense of being the 'good ones,' the majority, no longer strangers in their own land." — Arlie Russell Hochschild, Strangers in Their Own Land

"Our belief in inextricable human connection is one of our most renewable sources of courage ... I can stand up for what I believe is right when I know that regardless of the pushback and criticism, I'm connected to myself and others in a way that can't be severed. When we don't believe in an unbreakable connection .... we stay in our factions and echo chambers." — Brené Brown, Braving the Wilderness

For Better, For Worse: The Influence of Parents and Mentors

Our views are shaped, not only by the pain of our loved ones, but by the moral guidance we get from people we admire (and the moral pressure we feel and resent from people we dislike.)

When I was a young child, a man whom I greatly disliked — I'll call him Mr. Hyde, since that isn't his name — visited my parents for a few days. One day when I was supposed to be napping in my upstairs bedroom, and was actually lying with my ear to the floor to hear what the grown-ups were talking about, Mr. Hyde started talking about his black professional colleagues. (Mr. Hyde was white.) He said that they were underqualified and felt a huge sense of entitlement, and always got their way by claiming people were discriminating against them. I was too young to have any clear view of race relations, and I took this as another puzzling-but-true piece of information from the mysterious world of adults. "So that's what those people are like," I thought. "Huh, I didn't know that." Then I heard my mother telling Mr. Hyde, in the low and controlled tones which I knew expressed extreme displeasure, that she expected him never to make such false and offensive statements again in her house or in front of her children. "So it's not like that," I thought, "and Mama's telling him." Thereafter, I was predisposed to think of people who made explicitly racist arguments as being rude and annoying people like Mr. Hyde and their opponents as being delightful and admirable people like my mother.

But there's no clear correlation between loving parenting or good manners and antiracism. In his book, *The Making of a Racist,* Southern historian Charles Dew describes growing up with a mother he deeply loved and admired, both as a boy and a man. He knew her to be loving and thoughtful in both senses of the word — and she passed on to him the clear and deep belief that black people were fundamentally different and inferior. When he came to know black fellow students at college and started to question the view of race he'd inherited from his family, he felt profoundly disloyal to his mother and the other adults he loved and trusted.

Children who resent their parents may turn against parental political convictions with the same visceral intensity. Tony McAleer, a former neo-

Nazi who now works trying to help get others out of extremist groups, described his descent into extremism as partly a reaction to his father. McAleer senior believed in the importance of diversity, tolerance and courtesy. He also cheated on his wife rather publicly and ignored his son except for furious outbursts provoked by his son's outspoken admiration for Hitler. "What's the opposite of love?" McAleer asked rhetorically in an interview. "I'd rather have had bad attention from my dad than none at all."[45]

Longing to Belong

"Loneliness is not the sickness unto death. No, but can it be cured except by death? And does it not become the harder to bear the closer one comes to death?"
— Dag Hammarskjold, *Markings*, 1966

Our convictions are also shaped by our wish to belong. We are social animals; we fear isolation and seek connection. In *The Righteous Mind*, Jonathan Haidt argues that we are hard-wired to seek connection to a larger whole, to lose our separate identities as we identify with a larger group. He describes the transition from thinking of ourselves as individuals and trying to advance our own interests, to thinking of ourselves as part of a larger whole and trying to do what serves the group, as "the hive switch." Religious ceremonies and fervent political movements can be highly effective in flipping the hive switch. In evolutionary terms, he makes the case that the "hive switch" gives us a competitive advantage — that groups with high levels of corporate dedication out-compete other groups. In ethical terms today, the hive switch has a complicated and ambivalent function. Haidt puts it this way, "We're not always selfish hypocrites. We also have the ability, under special circumstances, to shut down our petty selves and become like cells in a larger body, or like bees in a hive, working for the good of the group. These experiences are often among the most cherished of our lives, although our hivishness can blind us to other moral concerns. Our bee-like nature facilitates altruism, heroism, war, and genocide." [46]

These benefits and dangers are similar to those associated with the moral foundation *Loyalty*. But that is a thought-construct, and the hive switch is a felt phenomenon, an intense inner experience, driven by our bone-deep desire for belonging. Many writers and psychologists have described the deepest human fear as the fear of being alone. Loneliness is psychologically painful and it takes a toll on our physical health as well. Brené Brown summarized a study which looked at factors reducing life expectancy in this way, "Living with air pollution increases your odds of dying early by 5 percent. Living with obesity, 20 percent. Excessive drinking, 30 percent. And living with loneliness? It increases our odds of dying early by 45 percent."[47] She quotes neuroscientist John Cacioppo's observation, "To grow to adulthood [in] a social species [like] humans, is not to become autonomous and solitary, it's to become the one on whom others can depend. Whether we know it or not, our brain and biology have been shaped to favor this outcome ... Denying you feel lonely makes no more sense than denying you feel hunger."[48] We're born with this need to connect, to be part of a larger whole.

Haidt argues that this always means identifying with one subgroup in contrast to another. He states, "It would be nice to believe that we humans were designed to love everyone unconditionally. Nice, but rather unlikely from an evolutionary perspective. Parochial love—love within groups—amplified by similarity, a sense of shared fate, and the suppression of free riders, may be the most we can accomplish."[49]

Brown, who is not theorizing based on evolution, but looking at studies in psychology, disagrees with the conclusion that love needs to be parochial. She also suggests that some forms of belonging are healthier for us than others, that some ways of trying to satisfy our hunger for belonging are nourishing while others are poisonous. And she asserts that the healthiest forms of belonging rest on a deep sense of the fundamental interconnectedness of all human beings.

In extreme cases this is clear to most of us. It's widely acknowledged that people who grow up feeling isolated are vulnerable to being seduced by extremist groups of all stripes which demand particularly high levels of commitment and offer a powerful sense of belonging based on a shared contempt for the rest of the world. The rest of the world rightly fears members of such groups and people who emerge from those groups often say afterward that the promise of belonging was illusory.

As I write, another example of this is just making news: Kevin Wilshaw, a British National Front activist and neo-Nazi, has left the movement and declared his contempt for it in a public interview. Wilshaw said he started joining nativist groups as a teenager, and skinhead groups as a young adult, because he didn't have many school friends and he just wanted to belong somewhere. He did find that sense of belonging. "Even though you end up being a group of people that through their own extreme views are cut off from society, you do have a sense of comradeship in that you're a member of a group that's being attacked by other people," he told the interviewer. But, he admitted, the relationships he built with comrades were false, because they were based on his hiding some important facts about himself — that he had some Jewish ancestry and that he was gay. When his comrades began to suspect he was gay, some of them became abusive. He said ruefully, "It's a terribly selfish thing to say but it's true, I saw people being abused, shouted at, spat at in the street — it's not until it's directed at you that you suddenly realise that what you're doing is wrong."[50]

But this false and ultimately unsatisfying sense of belonging isn't limited to extremist groups of one kind or another. As we saw in Chapter 2, ordinary Americans are increasingly sorting themselves by ideology: We live, worship, and interact online with people who share our views and avoid the others. This obviously makes it harder for members of different groups to understand and respect each other. University of Nebraska political scientist Elizabeth Theiss-Morse spoke to Bill Bishop, author of *The Big Sort*, about how confused people are by consensus they see in their neighborhoods versus the conflict they see at large in the nation. "People said many times, 'Eighty percent of us agree ... We all want the same thing ... It's those 20 percent who are just a bunch of extremists out there.' It didn't matter what their political views were. They really saw it as us against this fringe. The American people versus them, the fringe."[51] Or, as Rutgers state legislative specialist Alan Rosenthal put it, "If you live in a homogeneous community, you think, 'Everyone agrees this is right, so why the hell don't they do it?' Well, they don't do it because there is another homogeneous community over there that thinks quite the opposite. And candidates who come up through that [community] may also have less appreciation for democratic politics."[52]

The Devil Isn't in the Details: Idea Segregation

This sharp division is not solely — perhaps even primarily — a disagreement over policy specifics. Rather, it is a contrast between two overriding narratives about the world. Various studies have shown that American attitudes about abortion are becoming increasingly vehement and polarized. But when Americans are given, not a basic choice between pro-choice and pro-life, but a nuanced set of situational questions, most Americans actually fall into some kind of middle ground, considering abortion to be acceptable in some cases and not in others. As one book surveying religious attitudes put it, "the broad American public is not polarized on the specifics of the abortion issue. They believe that abortion should be legal but that it is reasonable to regulate it in various ways. They are 'pro-choice, buts'."[53]

They are, however, polarized on the framing narratives around abortion. One side talks almost exclusively about protecting the lives and liberty of women; the other about saving the lives of children. Indeed, one side generally insists on calling the being whose existence is terminated by abortion a baby, while the other side generally insists on calling it a fetus. And while both sides appeal to higher values, they often define those differently, with self-styled pro-lifers more often appealing to God's Will and God-given rights; self-styled pro-choicers to liberty, equality and human dignity.

In theory, it ought to be possible to combine concern for pregnant women and concern for the unborn, to make thoughtful compromises aimed at protecting both life and liberty. Bill Bishop describes a conversation with two Minnesota state lawmakers, Republican Duane Benson and Democrat Tim Penny: "Benson recalled how he and a Democratic legislator had put together the rarest of laws, a compromise on abortion. 'The bill would have reduced the number of abortions, but it would also have guaranteed rights,' Benson said. 'We thought naively that we had the formula. It was a wonderful experience and we went through the while process and we got two votes. His and mine. Because everyone else was pulled to their base.' Penny, suddenly excited, said, 'Now get this. Their proposal would have measurably decreased the number of abortions in Minnesota, and it would not have made abortion illegal. But they couldn't get support from either extreme.' There was a bit of silence, and then Benson said, 'What we have today is idea segregation'." [54]

Sometimes this idea segregation leads us to deny the possibility of middle ground. Brené Brown describes growing up in a conservative family that owned guns for hunting. She and her siblings got BB guns at an early age and learned to hunt with real weapons by the time they were in fifth grade. They also were rigorously drilled on gun safety (and forbidden to watch violent TV of any kind.) As Brown grew up, she was puzzled by the fact that her family seemed to support the NRA as its focus shifted from protecting the rights of hunters to encouraging the ownership of handguns for "self-defense" and opposing gun safety regulations which Brown saw as parallel to her family's safety rules. As an adult, Brown spoke to a largely liberal group at a conference and mentioned teaching her son to shoot skeet. A furious group participant asked how Brown could be a gun-lover and NRA supporter, how she could oppose common-sense gun regulation in a time of so many mass shootings. Brown tried to explain that she did support gun control, didn't support the NRA, and also thought responsible gun ownership was legitimate. This didn't impress the group member: "She was so angry at this point. She spit out, 'You either support guns or you don't'." Brown reflected ruefully that the woman's comments reflected the larger polarization of the gun debate. "Today's NRA ... forces 'us versus them' language over and over. *Allow anyone to buy any type of gun and ammunition, when and wherever they want, or they will break down your door, take away your guns, crush your freedom, kill everyone you love, and put an end to the American way. They are after us. They are coming.* That's the biggest bunch of bullshit I've heard since someone told me, 'If you own a gun — any gun — you might as well be the one pulling the trigger in all of these terrible mass shootings.' No and no."[55]

Some years ago, I took part in a contentious conversation on sexual ethics at a church conference. The initial question had concerned the denomination's position on same-sex marriage, and had spun out into two broader competing narratives. One was about godly and decent behavior being assailed by a debauched and secular world. The other was about patriarchal oppression and brutal suppression of LGBTQ people in particular and of the beautiful gift of sexuality in general. One side spoke with contempt of people who engaged in or supported same-sex unions, the other spoke with contempt of people who supported a narrower view of marriage and who talked about abstinence and chastity as possible and desirable things. I said that I believed sexuality was a gift of God, beautiful and dangerous; that I understood it to be rightly expressed either in celibacy or in marriage and that I didn't see any reason to restrict the gender of the parties in a marriage. There was a small silence and the conversation picked up where it had left off. After the meeting, a couple of other women came up to me to say that they thought what I thought, but they didn't want to say so, because they didn't want to be seen as "on the wrong side" by people they valued. I think of that conversation now as President Trump's administration moves to roll back LGBTQ rights and I see media stories about Christians versus the LGBTQ community. I'm not sure where that leaves me as a celibate bisexual Christian who strongly supports marriage equality. I'm not sure where that leaves a lot of people who don't completely agree with either side's framing narrative. My reading suggests that people usually solve this tension by talking loudly about the beliefs that bind them to others in Their Group, whichever group that is, and keeping carefully silent about whichever convictions and identities don't fit the group narrative.

The Power and Peril of the Deep Story

Each group is held together by the desperate wish of its members to belong, and also by what Hochschild calls a "deep story," which she defines as follows: "A deep story is a feels-as-if story — it's the story feelings tell, in the language of symbols. It removes judgement. It removes fact. It tells us how things feel. Such a story permits those on both sides of the political spectrum to stand back and explore the subjective prism through which the party on the other side sees the world. And I don't believe we understand anyone's politics, right or left, without it. For we all have a deep story."[56]

There are several components of the deep story. One is a framing narrative about what's happening in this country. After many months with her Tea Party hosts, Hochschild tried writing up the national narrative she thought she was hearing from them. They read her attempt and told her she'd gotten it right.

She told a story about people waiting patiently under the hot sun in a very long, very slow-moving line. At the unseen head of the line, over the brow of the hill, was the American Dream, the good life. That good life included financial security, but also a sense of honor and pride. The people waiting knew that wasn't something you could just run up and snatch. They knew they had to wait patiently. But the line didn't seem to be moving at all — in fact, it sometimes seemed to be moving backward. And people kept getting waved up from the back, being allowed to cut ahead of them in the line. Black people, women, immigrants, refugees, public sector workers were all being allowed to get ahead, while the patient white native-born conservative private-sector men made no progress at all. And the line supervisor kept saying the line cutters deserve to get ahead, and implying that the others deserve to get left behind. He talked about how hard life had been for the line cutters, and how bravely they'd dealt with their struggles. Who talked about how hard life had been for the conservatives? Who praised them for what they'd done well? When did race and gender and religion and citizenship stop being points of honor? Where was there any hope?

Later in the book, Hochschild suggests to her conservative friends that liberals have a very different deep story. In that story "The Dream," the good life, isn't off over the hill. It's in the center of the group, in a public square which offers everything necessary — schools, parks, libraries, hospitals, museums, etc. The liberals telling this story feel they've helped to build that public square, and to welcome new people into it, because that's what public squares are for. But invaders have burst into the square, torn down parts of the public buildings and removed them to build their own McMansions ...

Both groups see their hard work being devalued or destroyed. Both feel that their country has been taken over by hostile forces — that they are strangers in their own land. Hochschild hoped that if both groups could understand this, they might approach each other with greater compassion.

I think our Deep Stories also give feels-true answers to two other important and dangerous questions: Who are we? and Who are They, those folks who don't agree with us?

So far as I can tell, the conservative deep story is: We are hardworking, clean-living, God-fearing citizens of this great nation. We honor the values and traditions that made America great, and we will not let them be destroyed. And the liberal deep story is: We are clear-headed, open-minded, open-hearted citizens of the world. We are working to undo the prejudices and injustices of a more ignorant age and to birth a republic that truly has liberty and justice for all.

These stories are different in emphasis, but the virtues they praise need not be incompatible. The real trouble begins with the story about Them.

The stories I hear about Them from the Right and the Left are opposed in some ways, eerily similar in others. Both sides seem to regard their opponents as made up of a small group of rich evil masterminds and a large group of low-minded and ignorant rabble. In the conservative story, the masterminds are the Liberal Elites, led by George Soros. The rabble allied with them are the moochers, the looters, the scroungers, the parasites — people who can't succeed by their own efforts and feel entitled to the fruits of others' labors. The Elites want to keep the moochers alive, entitled and unsuccessful, so the moochers will keep voting the Democratic ticket. In the liberal story, the masterminds are the One Percent at the top of the country's income scale, led by the Kochs. The rabble allied with them are the deplorables, the uneducated bigots who have no good qualities of their own to take pride in and so cling to their hatred of minorities, which allows them to feel superior to someone. The One Percent wants to keep the deplorables uneducated, bigoted and angry so that the deplorables will keep voting the Republican ticket.

These stories involve shaming the rabble on the other side. We seem willing, even eager, to do that when we feel they've shamed us first.

Hochschild wrote about becoming friends with a church leader named Madonna, a generally upbeat, generous, outgoing, courteous person. Hochschild was shocked to find that Madonna loved listening to Rush Limbaugh's invective-laden rants against liberals. When she asked why, Madonna started by saying she liked the way he went after "feminazis," "commie libs," etc. Rather than arguing, Hochschild kept listening. She wrote, "Finally we came to Madonna's basic feeling that Limbaugh was defending her against insults she felt liberals were lobbing at her: "Oh, liberals think Bible-believing Southerners are ignorant, backward, redneck losers. They think we're racist, sexist, homophobic, and maybe fat."[57]

I've felt that same impulse to shake shame off myself by lobbing it back at the other person. I'm fairly thick-skinned about some things. I can handle being criticized for excessive liberalism or excessive conservatism. I can deal with people who think that I'm not a real Christian, or who think Christians are ignorant and delusional. But I don't deal at all well with the conservative story about liberal moochers/parasites. That's because I'm on Medicaid. My "day job" is as a full-time volunteer at a charitable organization where I get room and board in exchange for work. I do freelance work on evenings and weekends to earn money for other needs. But I can't afford health care, so the state foots the bill for my health insurance. In my considered opinion, I am contributing appropriately to society and not taking more than my share, but I am still uncomfortably aware that my health care is being paid for by people who didn't want to pay and are in many cases resentful, and I feel ashamed of that.

I've struggled to handle that shame constructively as I listen to my newly-elected Congresswoman and her supporters. She often draws a distinction between her real constituents — hardworking taxpaying people who support her — and the irresponsible paid protestors who disagree with her and aren't real constituents. She also favors cutting Medicaid dramatically; she says that her real constituents are being robbed to pay for unnecessary health care, and a drastically cut program would still serve all the people who really need it. As she lays out her criteria, I realize that to her I am not a real constituent, a hard worker, or a person in real need of health care. Some of her enthusiastic supporters on social media express their rage over how hard-working Americans are being sucked dry by the leeches of the welfare state. By their definition, I'm one of those leeches. Reading their words, I feel shamed and queasy. Sometimes I flip into fury. At that point, it's easy for me to forget that I value civil discourse and that I believe there's goodness in everyone and my job is to look for it. I nod and reach for the "like" button when people post savage verbal attacks on my Congresswoman. I snigger and read the uncomplimentary stories about prominent anti-welfare-state advocates instead of shaking my head and scrolling on by. I am ashamed of doing that, too, but that doesn't always stop me.

I have felt a little differently about my Congresswoman since I actually met her. I attended a public meeting where she spoke. I took notes, waved protest signs at moments when she staked out positions that troubled me and thank-you signs at moments when I agreed with her, and was pleasantly surprised to hear her making civil remarks about some constituents who disagree with her. Afterward, I went through a reception line to meet her. I thanked her for speaking more civilly of her opponents during the meeting and said I hoped she'd keep up that tone. "Please remember," I told her, "that we're also real people who want what's best for our neighbors, even if we see it differently. There are plenty of good people who have different opinions."

"But not everyone is good," she said, leaning forward. She started speaking bitterly about the fact that she had received death threats. I believe that to be true — it seems that in this country today politicians, journalists, and others in prominent positions are likely to receive death threats almost as a matter of routine, but that doesn't necessarily make it any easier to take. I made sympathetic noises. My Congresswoman went on to say that her opponent in the upcoming election was making what she described as personal attacks on her. I asked about some of the personal remarks she had made about him and his relatives during the meeting that had just concluded. She leaned further forward and actually started to shout, "Look what they're doing to me! I'm just protecting myself from these people! They have no shame! I'm just doing what I have to do!"

I left in a hurry, but I have thought about that since. I no longer think she's an Evil Mastermind coldheartedly manipulating people through their worst instincts. I think she's afraid or ashamed and acting out of defensiveness, a thing I've often done — and a thing all of us seem to be doing more and more often as polarization escalates. I think more kindly of her now, and I take a harder look at myself when I begin to slide into shame-based shaming.

It Gets Lonesome in the Bunker

This polarization and mutual shaming doesn't just make democracy and cross-divide communication more difficult. It also leaves us lonelier, even within our own groups. When we're brought together by our contempt for the Others, we're likely to feel the need to prove that we're not like the Others in any way, which may mean denying parts of our own experience and convictions. This rapidly becomes a self-reinforcing cycle. Bill Bishop notes, "When a person learns that others in the group share his or her general beliefs, he or she finds it socially advantageous to adopt a position slightly more extreme than the group average. It's a safe way to stand out from the crowd. It brings notice and even approbation." [58] Of course, after one person has done this, the next person looking for approbation has to move a little further toward the edge.

I have seen some of this pushing to extremes and in-group suspicion in an online group of my Congresswoman's progressive constituents which I joined after the last election. We came together to try to push back on a policy agenda we saw as destructive, but different members of the group prioritized different issues. Dispute over that sometimes grew rancorous, as people within the group who took more moderate positions on certain issues were accused of being Republicans or Russian trolls. Animosity also came up between those who felt that the important thing was to strengthen the Democratic Party and those who felt that the important thing was to reform the Democratic Party. Sometimes the former group was accused of being practically indistinguishable from Republicans; the latter of being covert Republicans undermining party unity. The bitterness might be less if we stopped using "Republican" as a term of contempt ... but trying to speak up for bipartisan unity also outrages some group members who feel that not condemning Republicans is tantamount to condemning minorities.

When this sort of push to the extremes takes place, some people blow up and leave, and more people quietly edit themselves to remain acceptable to their group. This self-censorship looks less dramatic than the explosive conflicts, but it also comes at a high price. It's difficult to have genuine and satisfying relationships when we are constantly editing ourselves to make sure we don't get cast out of the group. Perhaps this explains the simultaneous rise of polarization and of loneliness in our culture.

Brown writes, "Wouldn't you think that all the sorting by politics and beliefs we've been doing would lead to more social interaction? If we've hunkered down ideologically and geographically with people who we perceive to be just like us, doesn't that mean that we've surrounded ourselves with friends and people with whom we feel deeply connected? Shouldn't, 'You're either with us or against us,' have led to closer ties among the like-mined? The answer to these questions is a resounding and surprising *no*. **At the same time sorting is on the rise, so is loneliness.**"[59][Emphasis hers] She cites the data showing that in 1976, 25% of Americans lived in counties that gave a landslide victory to one presidential candidate, but in 2016 that figure had risen to 80%. Meanwhile, in 1980, about 20% of Americans described themselves as lonely, and that number is now above 40%. She notes that rates of self-reported loneliness are also rising in many other countries. It's in this context that she makes the observation I quoted at the beginning of this book: "The world feels high lonesome and heartbroken to me right now. We've sorted ourselves into factions based on our politics and ideology. We've turned away from one another and toward blame and rage. We're lonely and untethered. And scared. So damn scared."[60]

There is a way out of this fear and loneliness, but it's not an easy way. We have to stop stuffing our loneliness, our hunger to belong, with the toxic empty calories of blame and rage. We have to recognize that bunkers are no substitute for community. We have to redefine what it means to belong.

Brown writes about two true and paradoxical forms of belonging. The first is belonging to yourself, learning to set your own standards instead of looking to some larger group for validation. Maya Angelou gave a short, strong definition of this kind of belonging in a 1973 interview with Bill Moyers. Here's a bit of that interview:

ANGELOU: "You are only free when you realize you belong no place — you belong every place — no place at all. The price is high. The reward is great ... "

MOYERS: "Do you belong anywhere?"

ANGELOU: "I haven't yet."

MOYERS: "Do you belong to anyone?"

ANGELOU: "More and more. I mean, I belong to myself. I'm very proud of that. I am very concerned about how I look at Maya. I like Maya very much. I like the humor and courage very much. And when I find myself acting in a way that isn't ... that doesn't please me — then I have to deal with that.[61]"

But this doesn't mean giving up on community; on true connection with other people. Brown writes:

"Belonging to ourselves means being called to stand alone—to brave the wilderness of uncertainty, vulnerability, and criticism. And with the world feeling like a political and ideological combat zone, this is remarkably tough. We seem to have forgotten that even when we're utterly alone, we're connected to one another by something greater than group membership, politics and ideology — that we're connected by love and the human spirit. No matter how separated we are by what we think and believe, we're part of the same spiritual story."[62]

Truly believing that and having the courage to act on it is the key to freedom.

Learning some practices that make it easier to approach people who seem very different and to find common ground helps bring us closer to that freedom. That's what the next section is for.

Part 2: Building Bridges

Chapter 5

Preparing the Ground

"Wanting to reform the world without discovering one's true self is like trying to cover the world with leather to avoid the pain of walking on stones and thorns. It is much simpler to wear shoes." — Sri Ramana Maharshi

"First take the plank out of your own eye, and then you will see clearly to remove the speck from your brother's eye." — Matthew 7:5, New International Version

Self-Knowledge

Before we can engage people across the aisle in meaningful dialogue, we need to be ready to listen well. That doesn't mean that political dialogue needs to be put off until all our own prejudices, fears, traumas and blind spots are dealt with. For one thing, we need a more constructive political dialogue now, not years in the future; for another, we may only become aware of some of our prejudices, fears, traumas and blind spots by talking with people who don't share them. But we have a better chance of reaching constructive dialogue if we've made some attempt to prepare the ground by understanding and accepting ourselves, and by strengthening our faith in our own inherent goodness and that of other people.

Roshi Joan Halifax teaches, "All too often, our so-called strength comes from fear, not love.; instead of having a strong back, many of us have a defended front shielding a weak spine. In other words, we walk around brittle and defensive, trying to conceal our lack of confidence. If we strengthen our backs, metaphorically speaking, and develop a spine that's flexible but sturdy, then we can risk having a front that's soft and open."[63]

Strengthening our backs requires us to look closely at our convictions and the stories and experiences that formed them. Once we understand the roots of our convictions, we're less likely to fear that someone else's argument will destroy our beliefs and leave us disoriented. We're more likely to be open to reevaluating some of our conclusions — finding other ways to understand and express the deepest values and loves which gave rise to them. The first section of this book offers some ways of looking at the forces which shape our convictions. You will think of others. The important thing is to look carefully and not to be afraid of what you see. Halifax added, "How can we give and accept care with strong-back, soft-front compassion, moving past fear into a place of genuine tenderness? I believe it comes about when we are truly transparent, seeing the world clearly—and letting the world see us."[64]

How to enter that place of true transparency would have to be the subject of a longer and more in-depth book. Various spiritual traditions offer ways into that openness. So do various schools of psychotherapy. Brown's book, *Braving the Wilderness,* offers suggestions not framed in the context of any particular religious or clinical tradition. I think the courage to look is the main requirement; once we have that, we can figure out the rest.

Strengthening our backs also requires us to let go our fear that if we open our minds we will cease to belong and will be left lonely. This may be a difficult task, because on the surface level this fear can appear to be justified.

Over and over in my life I've struggled with the tension between my wish to belong in groups and my wish to befriend people perceived as outsiders by the group. I left one church whose congregation matched my theology and political concerns well and was eager to work for peace and justice. I left partly because they were clearly not interested in welcoming or thinking about working-class people or conservatives. (I had started to get this sense in subtler ways, but it became quite evident when a church leader said of a newcomer, "He talks as though he has no education and he works at Price Chopper, and last week I heard him say something pro-Bush. I don't know what he's doing here," and other people clucked and shook their heads. Another leader added that her family were conservatives to who she couldn't talk and she came to this church to be with people who weren't like that.) I left another church, a small working-class congregation whose members showed a deep love and connection with God and each other, when the pastor began to preach on how the horrors which the Jews have suffered over the past two thousand years were God's punishment for their rejection of Christ. After the 2016 election, as I mentioned in Chapter 4, I joined an online group of progressives trying to organize to protect health coverage for low-income folks, civil rights for immigrants, higher refugee admissions etc. I found many helpful resources and much encouragement in that group, but when I spoke of hearing some legitimate concerns from my conservative friends I was told that I was promoting false equivalencies just like the people who justified Hitler. I had a conservative friend and neighbor who visited my farm often (with mutual satisfaction), until the 2016 election happened. He began talking about the need to protect the country from dangerous foreigners and I began talking about the refugees and other immigrants I knew, admired and loved. I still invite him, but he no longer comes to visit.

Those are real losses, but they aren't the whole story. When I left the churches, I retained valued friendships with members of the congregation — and also a strong sense of still being part of the broken body of Christ along with the folks in the groups I'd left and the folks in the groups they feared. I still have and treasure friendships with friends on different ends of the political spectrum. I don't have to feign agreement with these friends. We have learned — not always comfortably — to love each other even as we disagree. And I remain convinced that we are all bound together by this fragile beautiful planet we share, by the intricate and invisible connections of the global economy, and also in a deeper oneness. As a character in a short story by Wendell Berry says, "The way we are, we are members of each other. All of us. Everything. The difference ain't in who is a member and who is not, but in who knows it and who don't."[65] I'm trying to more consistently know and remember my membership. And to practice the useful technique described in Edwin Markham's poem, *Outwitted*:

> "He drew a circle that shut me out--
>> Heretic, a rebel, a thing to flout.
> But Love and I had the wit to win:
>> We drew a circle that took him in!"

When I remember that, I am able to go out and meet other people where they are without defensiveness. I'm able to listen deeply to what they say, rather than skimming their words for refutable arguments. I'm able to say what I mean without falsifying in fear of losing a friend, or overstating in fear of being insufficiently righteous.

And when I forget, when I soft-pedal or snap, when I realize I've treated someone as an enemy rather than a friend who disagrees, I try to apologize. I try to see where the wound is in me that made it so hard for me to respond well, and to tend that wound. I try, next time someone snaps at or dismisses me, to remember that they're probably wounded, too, and to have some patience.

Seeking Diverse Perspectives

Some people find it helpful to start by reading news, analysis and stories from another perspective so that they can begin to imagine the other side's deep story before being caught in the midst of a difficult conversation. The distance, safety and time for thought which this allows can be advantageous. But go cautiously, and don't rely exclusively on reading. The loudest voices at either end of the spectrum may not be good representatives of the ordinary people who populate each side of the political divide. Liberal writer Arlie Russell Hochschild started her attempt to understand conservatives by reading Ayn Rand and listening to Rush Limbaugh. She traveled to Tea Party country with some trepidation, expecting to hear the same vitriol from conservatives on the ground that she heard from Limbaugh and Rand, and she was surprised by the friendliness, openness and good humor of her Tea Party hosts — even those who were Limbaugh admirers.

Check out news sources that view current events through a different framing narrative than the one you're used to. Allsides.com offers left-leaning, centrist and right-leaning perspectives on a variety of issues from somewhat mainstream news sources. (Granted, people disagree about what's left-leaning and right-leaning. Allsides asks users to describe their own political leanings, then to describe their perception of the leanings of various news articles and news sources, and Allsides uses those user rankings to drive their ratings.) They also offer a discussion platform which requires users to start by pledging civility. Red Feed, Blue Feed (described in Chapter 2), lets you search for different issues and find left- and right-leaning headlines trending on Facebook. These tend to be much more extreme, and to derive from more marginal sources, than Allsides' articles. If you're trying to understand the legitimate concerns of people who disagree with you, and to get well-written pieces from reputable sources that don't match your preconceptions, Allsides may be a good place to start. If you find a news source from the other side there that strikes you as well-written, you might want to follow that site yourself. If you're interested in observing the mirrored escalating rhetoric on either side, Red Feed, Blue Feed can be eye-opening. Avoid selecting the most reasonable narratives on your side and the most extreme narratives on the other side.

Try reading books written from the other side. This will back you away from the constant drama of the headlines and give you a deeper feel for underlying narratives and themes. If you have any friends of the other political persuasion, ask them for book recommendations. If not, see if you can find any books from the other side that got somewhat respectful reviews from someone on your side. If you don't find that, just try reading several different authors. If a particular author inspires you with nothing but disgust, drop them and keep trying others until you find something you can respect, if not agree with. (I wish I had taken this advice to heart before making myself read through to the bitter end of *Atlas Shrugged*. Oh, well ...)

Pay attention to your frame of mind as you read. Reading with an eye to refutable arguments, offensive statements, etc., can add to your arsenal in a debate, or to the outrage about Those People that you share with your group, but it's not likely to help you understand another perspective more fully. My experience so far, and the articles I've read, suggest that the ammunition thus gathered is not apt to make any dent in the certainty of your neighbor or relative who strongly disagrees with you. Try to read with an open mind. Listen for anything that you can affirm; for anything that raises an echo in your own mind and heart.

The point is not to ignore or deny deep disagreements, but to look for what else is there. Sometimes, I have been able to sympathize with some of an author's underlying concerns even as I disagree strongly with their ideas of the right solution. While reading Glenn Beck's novel, *The Overton Window*, I kept alternating between nodding and glaring at the book. I understood and shared his looking back with longing to a simpler time when people were able and willing to do the physical work to provide for their own needs, and when they knew their neighbors well and took care of them. I was puzzled by his assumption that it's Big Government, not the rise of global consumer capitalism, that stands against this model. I was also extremely skeptical of his implying that overtly bigoted or violent members of far-right groups were actually agents provocateurs planted by the Left, but at least there was some point of connection. I read Peter Brimelow's anti-immigration tract, *Alien Nation*, in a much less promising frame of mind; looking for refutable arguments as I prepared a pro-immigration tract of my own. I was shocked by much of Brimelow's argument and found it worth opposing. But underneath the assumptions of ethnic superiority (which I find deeply offensive) and the assertion that homogeneity brings peace (which I find directly contradictory to historical evidence), I heard what I took to be a genuine love and fear for his young son — a longing for there to be some safe place for the boy to grow up in. If I ever had the chance to speak to Brimelow, I would try to acknowledge that love and fear and suggest a different way of dealing with it.

When Not to Talk

It's important to reach out and communicate across divides. It's also important to recognize when this isn't a good idea.

Sometimes we're really not ready to talk yet. If we're trapped inside our own pain or outrage, we're not ready to talk with people who disagree — we're likely to lacerate them and ourselves if we try. If we flash into fury whenever we read a news story written from another perspective, we're probably not ready for a conversation yet. We need to sit with that pain and anger and see where it comes from. It may not go away. It may not need to. But we need to understand it, to own it, and to understand that other people may have similarly fraught responses to stories and statements that we hold dear. Until we can do that, we're better off not trying to start a controversial dialogue.

This isn't a linear process in which we get better every day in every way. When we're tired, or ill, or feeling scraped raw by some private pain, our ability to reach across divides constructively may be diminished. When we feel desperately lonely or dissatisfied with ourselves, we won't have much energy and resilience left over for building bridges.

Sometimes the other person may not be ready to talk. If you say something and the other person explodes, this may indicate that they've got more of their own work to do before they're ready to talk with you. Try to say something that shows that you care about their distress — , that you don't want to exacerbate it, that you haven't changed your mind, and that you'd be glad to try talking about the issue sometime when they're feeling better. Try not to start fraught conversations with other people who are obviously tired, ill, or feeling scraped raw by some private pain.

Sometimes the relationship isn't right for a conversation. If you're trying to sort out difficult personal and family issues with a relative or friend, it may be wise to set politics aside until you've come to some peace with the more close and visceral issues. I have not seen good results from attempts to discuss politics while taking care of a very sick loved one or while at a funeral. (Yes, I have seen political discussions flare up in both settings. That's all I have to say about that ...)

It's important to reach out to people who are different from you, and to be willing to accept some discomfort in the process. But it's also important to set boundaries that protect your safety.. Physical safety matters, of course. It's not helpful to start a discussion with someone who's liable to haul off and hit you. Emotional safety is also a real concern, and is very different from emotional comfort. Different people will have different boundaries. The important thing is to be clear about where yours are, and to respect other people's boundaries when we state them.

The issue of boundaries itself has become somewhat politically polarizing, as people on the Right complain of the Left demanding "safe spaces." It's true that people on either side can sometimes set conversational boundaries that leave a lot of people out or prevent real discussion of the issue at hand. I finally stopped trying to correspond with a conservative friend who insisted that there was no point in talking with anyone so dishonest and degraded as to disagree with the self-evident statement that Christianity was fundamentally opposed to all other religions. I've dropped conversations with liberal friends who insisted that anyone who disagreed with their position on transgender issues was hateful and needed to shut up. Friends have told me that it's hard to communicate with me because I tend to get upset and shut the conversation down over what I see as scapegoating and they see as reasonably pointing out the damage done by certain groups of people.

But it's also true that we don't know what traumas may raise other people's requirements for emotional safety, and we'd better tread carefully. I have a friend who told me that she voted for Trump partly because he stood up to the culture of entitlement and political correctness which led to college students demanding safe spaces with puppies and cookies whenever anyone disagreed with them. That story was new to me. I asked for details, which she didn't have. I Googled "college safe spaces puppies cookies" and came up with a story about a debate over sexual assault hosted at a college which also offered a designated "safe space" with comfort objects — and also with trained counselors on standby for students who had been sexually assaulted and might experience flashbacks or trauma during the debate.[66] I told my friend that. She said (unhappily) that she hadn't known that was the issue. My friend had tried to comfort and support another friend who was raped at college, and she believed that women who'd undergone that experience might well need support and comfort when rape was being discussed. So ... know your vulnerabilities, do what it takes to keep yourself safe, and don't push past other people's boundaries just because you don't understand why they're there.

Brown suggested that dehumanizing language and behavior violate emotional safety, and that it's best not to stay engaged with people who repeatedly engage in dehumanization — referring to people who aren't like them as somehow subhuman, or expressing the belief that those people aren't entitled to basic human rights. I see the danger in dehumanization. I know that genocides generally begin with dehumanizing language, calling Those People "untermenschen" (racially and/or socially inferior) or "cockroaches" or ... I know that I react with shame and fury to being called a "welfare leech." I have enough empathy and imagination so that I also object vehemently and feel similar outrage when I hear dehumanizing racial slurs used against other people, or when I hear others being called "fascist pigs," "lawless animals," or "racist pieces of shit."

This doesn't necessarily mean that we can't talk with people whose basic convictions we find deeply offensive; even with people who do seem to assume that other groups are less than fully human. I've been reading stories of people who exit hate groups after enthusiastically participating in a dehumanizing narrative, and I see that often a transforming factor is actually interacting with people from the group they've dehumanized — people who understand the hate they're up against and keep speaking to their fellow human being trapped inside the hate. I am thinking of Daryl Davis, the black musician who convinced more than two hundred members of the Ku Klux Klan to give up their robes and leave the group. His first encounter was with a listener at one of his concerts who came up to him and had a civil conversation before revealing that he was in the KKK. Davis decided to keep talking with him. After that Davis sought out other Klan members and approached them one by one, asking, "How can you hate me when you don't even know me?" Some of them answered him by explaining that they just knew black people had smaller brains, violent genes, etc., that they were less than fully human. Davis managed to respond matter-of-factly ... and, in time, many of them came around.[67] He wasn't the first one to do this. Civil rights activist Xernona Clayton spent a year having difficult conversations with a Klan leader she met through a civic group. He appeared to be laughing off everything she said, but at the end of that time he left the white supremacy movement.[68]

But this approach is dangerous, demanding, and not for everyone. It's important to know where your boundaries are; what you can handle without falling into shame and fury. It's also important to know what is likely to trigger traumatic memories, and it's fine to set boundaries to save yourself from being needlessly hurt. A little trial and error will probably make this clear. Know your boundaries, stick to them, and state them clearly.

Chapter 6

Stepping Out, Finding Common Ground

"The English language doesn't give us many words to describe the feeling of reaching out to someone from another world, and of having that interest welcomed. Something of its own kind, mutual, is created. What a gift. Gratitude, awe, appreciation; for me all these words apply ..." — Arlie Russell Hochschild, *Strangers in Their Own Land*

The next step into understanding is actually getting to know people who live on the other sides of our deepening political and cultural divides. I've sometimes taken this step for granted, as I'm a liberal (more or less) living in a conservative (more and more) area, and I'm also a member of an intentional community that hosts guests from across the political spectrum. But I often hear from my friends on either side that they just don't know anyone (except, sometimes, me) who doesn't share their political convictions. And, as Chapters 2 and 4 describe, studies suggest that more and more Americans are living in echo chambers, not interacting much with people who have a different deep story.

Liberal writer Arlie Russell Hochschild described the importance of reaching across what she called "the empathy wall." She wrote at the beginning of her book, "An empathy wall is an obstacle to deep understanding of another person, one that can make us feel indifferent or even hostile to those who hold different beliefs or whose childhood is rooted in different circumstances. In a period of political tumult, we grasp for certainties. We shoehorn new information into ways we already think. We settle for knowing our opposite numbers from the outside. But is it possible, without changing our beliefs, to know others from the inside, to see reality through their eyes, to understand the links between life, feeling, and politics; that is, to cross the empathy wall? I thought it was."[69]

Thinking that, Hochschild spent a long time visiting and *listening to* people on the far side of her empathy wall — Tea Party supporters, enthusiastic proponents of deregulation, who lived in a part of Louisiana poisoned by industrial waste. From the beginning, she could see that they were in a difficult situation, but their response to that situation made no sense to her. She noted that she could see what they were missing, but couldn't yet see what she was missing. She kept listening As she got to know them as whole people — to feel their loves and fears and memories, until the empathy wall finally came down — she was able to picture and resonate with their deep story about what's true. As she did this, some of them seemed to get a warmer and more positive sense of the possibilities inherent in liberals.

There are several ways to reach across the divide, to put yourself in contact with Those People. Different approaches will likely work for different temperaments.

Brené Brown writes about the importance of sharing strongly felt human experiences with strangers who may not be like you. She doesn't suggest starting this by holding political discussions with them. She does recommend taking part in large events that gather people from across the political spectrum to laugh and cry and get excited together. Brown mentions sports games (this was before the controversy about demonstrations during the playing of the national anthem before sporting events), movies, theater performances, and concerts; she describes music as "the most powerful form of collective joy."[70] In Jonathan Haidt's terms from Chapter 1, these are events that flip the hive switch, that get us feeling and acting like members of a larger body instead of isolated individuals. These experiences can relieve the pressure of loneliness that make us seek comfort in like-minded bunker groups. They can also serve as reminders of our shared humanity. (Brown acknowledges that there's also a danger in events that flip the hive switch while encouraging us to feel bonded to each other against those enemies over there.)

Brown is an extrovert. Many of my outgoing friends seem to be strengthened, renewed and energized by being part of a large pumped-up crowd. I don't thrive in these contexts; I find people delightful in small numbers and overwhelming in crowds. Not because I think somebody's going to mug me, but because I am used to noticing each person around me as an individual and I simply get worn-out thinking, "There's a tall man with a sad face that twitches a little. There's a weathered-looking woman with her feet tight together trying to see over his shoulder. There's a guy with an armful of fliers I can't read from this angle. There's a kid with earbuds in singing along to something I can't hear ..." And when I'm in a highly excited crowd, part of me shares in the excitement, but a voice in the back of my head shouts, "THEY'RE MANIPULATING YOUR EMOTIONS! THEY"RE MESSING WITH YOUR MIND! DON'T LET THEM!" This also is tiring.

There are other approaches for introverts. Smaller groups focused on doing something together can offer a less overwhelming and more personal experience of shared emotion. I'm part of a contradance group that draws a very wide range of people together to move to music. The book discussion group at my local library draws a diverse group of people together to imagine their way into the joys and sorrows of strangers. Brown also writes about going to funerals — being with people in their grief, —as a powerful practice of empathy and unity.

Shared volunteer activities can also form strong connections that cross divides. Obviously, volunteering for a political cause will most likely bring you together with like-minded people. But people who can't agree on public policy matters can still get together to clean up a park or a street, cook and clean up at a soup kitchen, do yard work for elders or home repair for low-income folks. As you work, you'll have a chance to talk about the day-to-day details of your lives and get to know each other as real people. And shared volunteering tends to build respect and trust. It's hard to dismiss the person who's helping you put a patch on someone's leaking roof as a heartless hypocritical Republican or a lazy irresponsible Democrat. If and when tense political discussions do arise in the group, you'll have some shared esteem to help carry you through the difficulty.

There's also a place for deliberately gathering with the intention of discussing divisive issues.

Interfaith discussion groups can help you to understand the deep stories of people with very different religious convictions. In-person groups are best, because there's a richness in hearing people's voices, seeing their faces, holding their hands, which can't be replicated online. But for people who live, as I do, in remote and somewhat religiously homogeneous areas, online interfaith discussions can also be rewarding. Choose a group that's set up for discussion not debate, a group with clear rules which promote civility and consistent moderators who hold the group accountable to those standards. I've found that such groups can offer a chance to understand other faiths better, and to bring together liberal and conservative members of any given faith in ways that are uncomfortable and productive. The best online group I've been part of deepened its sense of community by encouraging members to offer prayer requests and to pray for each other. It's much harder to look down on or suspect someone who's prayed for you, or whom you've prayed for, in the midst of illness or job loss or grief.

The Living Room Conversations Project offers resources and guidance for deliberate conversations across the political divide. They provide ground rules, background readings and suggested questions for discussion. They urge people to volunteer in pairs — one liberal, one conservative — to host a discussion in one of the facilitators' homes or in a small, comfortable public space. Up to eight other people (hopefully evenly divided between sides), come together for an in-depth discussion involving a great deal of listening, asking clarifying questions, and telling the stories at the roots of their convictions. Living Room Conversations also organizes live chats online, though they strongly recommend meeting in person whenever that's possible. Larger open forums with the same idea; beginning with shared meals and personal conversation and continuing into civil political discussion across party lines have been offered by the Make Shift Coffee House in Maine, which offers resources for other groups wishing to try something similar.

Allsides.com offers links to many other civil discussion resources and groups. For links and more information see the Appendix.

Meaningful conversations with strangers can also happen one-on-one. I've found public transportation to be a good incubator for such conversations. Once I started talking with a stranger on the Greyhound bus from Syracuse to Boston because he saw me fumbling with the seat belt and assured me that it really wasn't necessary. That led into talk about our experiences with public transportation, which became talk about the places we came from (he lived in the city, I'd always lived in small towns), and where we were headed. As I was going to a church conference, and he found religion intriguing but rather alien, we talked about God and the meaning of life for the next three hours. After the weekend, we met each other in the Boston bus station and continued the conversation all the way home. On another occasion, I spent two hours in an amiable debate over the ethics of genetic engineering — I think my interlocutor was en route to a science conference. More often, I've just had rambling personal conversations about kids and growing-up experiences, memories and worries and hopes. Those conversations have happened across race and religious and ideological gaps, and they've strengthened my sense that we all belong to one another.

I've also plunged into explicitly political conversations with strangers whom I recognized as from The Other Side. Once I did that online. Facebook, which continues to suggest that I like far-left pages, far-right pages and everything in between, suggested that I might like a small conservative blog. The post they featured that day was called, "Liberal Ideas: The New Looney Tunes." I glowered at the headline, reflected consolingly that Facebook's targeting mechanisms aren't as omniscient as some articles suggest, and went to scroll on by. But then I noticed several comments on the post expressing disappointment and dismay at the writers' lack of success in getting any liberals to talk civilly and thoughtfully with them about politics. I admit my first thought was, "That's probably because you present yourselves as thoughtless and uncivil jerks." Then I recognized how thoughtless and uncivil that thought was. Then I posted a comment saying that I was a liberal eager for opportunities for thoughtful and civil dialogue with conservatives, and I was pleasantly surprised by the courteous and substantive nature of some (not all) of the replies I received. The blog host even invited me to write guest posts, which I did.

There'll be more about that encounter in the next chapter. For now, I'll just note that there's a side benefit to online conversation with people who don't agree with you. I have sometimes been skeptical when people talked to me about the sinister influence of Big Data collection and the micro-targeting of online messages. "That sounds creepy," I've thought, "but Facebook is still alternately inviting me to like Bernie Sanders and Mike Pence. Those mechanisms don't really work very well." When I said something to that effect on Facebook, several friends said that FB targeted them consistently with ads for one side, and suggested that I saw a wider range of promoted posts because I had very conservative friends and not infrequently looked into the stories they recommended. I probably wouldn't have seen the conservative blog at all if I hadn't had, and regularly engaged in online conversation with, conservative Facebook friends. After following the blog page I received more suggested stories from the other side.

Early in President Obama's first term, I jumped into in-person cross-partisan conversation during a long wait for a train. I heard a young man and an older woman, both white, talking animatedly to each other about their struggle to balance their political passion with their fear of being arrested or attacked for speaking out. At least, I thought that was what they were saying. I said I'd overheard a bit of their conversation and wondered if it would be okay for me to join in, as I was trying to understand their perspective better. They seemed nonplussed, but agreed.

First, I just asked if I was hearing them correctly. They said yes, I was. The man —who I learned was the woman's grandson — said that Obama favored expanding the powers of big government, quite possibly to include suppressing free speech and jailing dissidents, though the man was still signing petitions. The woman said she'd heard stories about Obama secretly sending out thugs to beat conservatives up, so she'd stopped signing petitions. I blinked, swallowed hard, expressed sympathy for their fears, and said truthfully that they reminded me of some of my liberal activist friends who had expressed fears during Bush's presidency that the administration might be tapping their phones/might send them to Guantanamo Bay ... I added that I had not been a fan of Bush but I thought those fears were exaggerated, as I thought the fears of my present companions were. (I thought it prudent not to add that I had thought some —not all — of my liberal friends had enjoyed the feeling that their protests were effective enough to warrant a government crackdown.) The grandmother and grandson expressed shock that anyone would think a law-abiding president like Bush who exemplified American values would curb the First Amendment rights of American citizens. We talked a bit, gingerly, about what we each took American values to mean.

I don't believe we convinced each other of anything, but I think (I hope) that they came away believing that there were some honest and well-meaning (if misguided) liberals, and that I was one; perhaps, also, having a bit of compassion for frightened people on the other side. I really hope they didn't come away thinking I was a spy for President Obama who was going to send criminal enforcers after them. I suppose if they did think that, that the non-arrival of enforcers might eventually have soothed their fears ... Later, when I heard stories about other people's exaggerated fears of President Obama, instead of thinking "Those expletive-deleted racists," I remembered the grandmother and grandson — their affection for each other, their strong if puzzling convictions, and their palpable fears. I still thought those fears were misplaced, but I could sympathize. I struggle with anxiety and obsessive-compulsive tendencies; I know how irrational fears can assume nightmare proportions, block clear thought and suck the joy out of life.

That's one of Brené Brown's conclusions: We don't need to be able to share another person's memories or their cognitive framework in order to empathize with them. We simply need to recognize their emotions and to remember our own. Joy, pain, fear, grief, outrage, compassion — we've all experienced them. If we listen well, we can recognize them in each other.

Sometimes we avoid recognizing pain in others because we don't want to have to treat them as fully human. Sometimes we just don't want to have to face our own pain. Sometimes we're afraid of saying or doing the wrong thing. But the most important thing we can do for other people in their pain is to be there with them. To see them. Not to ignore them, not to try to fix them, but to be there and bear witness.

When we do that for other people, or when they do that for us, we can't help seeing each other as fully human, and caring for each other. That won't take away our political disagreements. But it will give us a solid foundation on which to build our bridges.

Chapter 7

Building Bridges

"The goal of an honest, respectful dialogue is to open our minds, not to change them." — Celeste Headlee, We Need to Talk

"Civility is claiming and caring for one's identity, ideas and beliefs without degrading someone else's in the process ... disagreeing without disrespect, seeking common ground as a starting point for dialogue about differences, listening past one's preconceptions, and teaching others to do the same. Civility is the hard work of staying present even with those with whom we have deep-rooted and fierce disagreements." — Brené Brown, Braving the Wilderness

So now you know where your boundaries are, you've encountered some people with different viewpoints who are up for a conversation, and you're ready to begin. There are no hard and fast rules for engaging in constructive conversation without exhausting or distressing yourself or your conversation partners. But there are a few basic principles and practices which may prove helpful, including the following:

Listening

Journalist Celeste Headlee noted ruefully in a TED Talk that, "we're talking more, and in more different ways, but we're not actually having conversations." The reason for this, she says, is that we are too often unwilling to actually listen. "If you can't do that, you're not having a conversation. You're just two people shouting out barely related sentences in the same space."[71] This describes a great deal of the political "conversation" I see online or hear on the radio — and, alas, too many in-person "conversations" in which I've participated.

How can we really listen?

We need to focus on our conversation partner. Headlee strongly recommends not trying to multitask while having a conversation. The examples she gives are mostly about trying to carry on multiple verbal tasks at once; to talk while texting, or emailing, or listening to the radio. These activities tend to dilute our focus, distract us from the other person, and decrease both our understanding of their arguments and our sense of rapport. Giving the other person our undivided attention can be a powerful thing. That recommendation makes sense to me, but I'd add from my own experience, that it can be helpful to have some kind of simple manual work to do — washing dishes, weeding a garden bed, painting a wall — while conversing. I know some people who find it extremely difficult to sit still, and who are better able to concentrate and listen if they have something to do with their hands. The act of working together can also strengthen a sense of having something in common. Other people prefer to talk when their eyes, hands and minds can be fully engaged in the conversation. Do what works for you and your partner, but be sure you really have attention to spare.

Focus means not only concentrating on the conversation, but concentrating on what the other person is saying while they're saying it. Too often, we use the other person's talking time to draft our own replies. Listen fully while the other person is talking. Be willing to pause after that and formulate your thoughts clearly. A little silence will do no harm. Too often, we listen to catch errors and offensive remarks which we perceive as putting the other person at a disadvantage. This doesn't facilitate true conversation. Headlee recommends coming into a conversation with the goal — not of changing the other person's mind or educating them — but of learning something about them. Andrés Miguel Rondón, the Venezuelan economist who wrote about the rise of Chavez and the dangers of polarization, suggests that the most important goal of conversation is to keep a human-level connection which stops people on either side from dehumanizing the Other.

We must be willing to be made uncomfortable. Headlee's interviewer asked if listening to morally repugnant remarks wasn't the same as condoning them; granting them legitimacy. Headlee pointed out that as polarization rises, people on both sides are increasingly likely to find each other's views morally repugnant. Silencing and shaming people decreases their exposure to alternative points of view and increases the bitterness of their internal narrative, which tends to have bad results in the long term. This certainly rings true to me. When I feel attacked and shut up, I am much less likely to question my own behavior than to blame the other person. And, I've come to see that listening to someone else is not tacitly consenting to their position, it's just treating them as a human being who is worth listening to.

Quiet listening can also have surprising results. Headlee quoted Xernona Clayton, the black civil rights activist who persuaded a Grand Dragon to leave the Klan. Clayton said, "I just listened to him."

I've never seen anything that dramatic. But I did hear about another conversation in which listening mattered. I live and work at a charitable nonprofit where we grow food to share with neighbors. One day during the Iraq war, an acquaintance (whom I'll call Grace) came to pick beans to can for her family. One of my fellow volunteers went up to the garden to pick with her. Grace seemed unhappy, and the volunteer asked what was going on. Grace said she was worried about one of her sons, who was deploying to Iraq with the Marines. The volunteer expressed concern and said she'd be praying for Grace and her son. Grace waxed voluble about how violent those Arab Muslims were, how grateful they ought to be that we were going in to take care of them, how ungrateful and untrustworthy they were. The volunteer listened quietly. Finally, Grace said, "You're not saying anything."

"I hope your son will be safe," the volunteer said. "This must be so hard."

Grace went back to talking about what was wrong with the Iraqis. Then she said again, "You're very quiet. You don't agree with me?"

"I know you're worried about your son," the volunteer said. "I don't want to argue with you. I'll pray for him."

"But how can you not agree with me?" Grace asked.

The volunteer said a little bit about what we had heard of the suffering caused in Iraq by the war. She then said that the U.S. also had problems, but we most likely wouldn't feel grateful if people of another faith and ethnicity came in with guns to set us right.

"Where do you hear things like that?" Grace asked. The volunteer said it didn't matter, but when Grace persisted she said a bit about our news sources — both formal and informal.

Grace made it clear that she hadn't known that good people who were like her —farmers, hard workers, Christian parents — could oppose the war. She wasn't changing her mind, but she'd heard the volunteer's concern for her and her son and she was willing to allow that, strange as it seemed to her, good people differed with her.

In situations where the stress isn't mostly on one side, listening and talking can be more mutual. But it's still important to listen closely to the other person as we want them to listen to us. Here are some ways of focusing that I've found helpful:

Listen for common ground. That doesn't mean denying or avoiding areas of disagreement. It does mean listening for the things that still unite us.

Listen for emotion. Pain, joy, affection, fear, anger ... You don't have to think the other person's feelings are reasonable; just recognize that they're having them, remember what that feels like, and respond accordingly. "I'm sorry you're so afraid. That can be exhausting," can be honestly said even when you think the fear is ill-founded. Listen for love. What does the other person care about? What are they trying to protect? You may be able to affirm that even when you strongly disagree with what they're doing in an attempt at protection. As I described earlier, anti-immigrant policies that appall me sometimes seem to be partly rooted in the speaker's passionate protective feelings for their children. It's possible to acknowledge that love and will to protect — even while suggesting that turning immigrants away doesn't necessarily make children safer, that immigrant parents also love their children and seek a safe place in which to raise them, etc., etc.

Listen for underlying differences. Not just their specific issue position, but what undergirds it. Listen for experiences. What are the other person's wounds, triumphs, failures?

Listen for values. What are the other person's moral foundations?

Asking Questions

Questions help the other person to see that you're listening, and help you to get a clearer grasp on what you're listening to.

Headlee recommends asking open-ended questions. She says the journalist's basic questions are also useful in daily conversations: Who, what, when, why, where, who? This allows the other person to speak in the framework that makes sense to them rather than trying to fit into your pigeonholes. It can also move them past the basic talking points they've heard and into a more thoughtful exploration. I find it particularly helpful, if a discussion is turning acrimonious, to ask questions that shift the mode from debate to storytelling. How did you come to believe this? How do you decide which news sources to trust? What's been your experience with migrants/law enforcement/getting the health care you need?

I learned this first as a defusing technique when I decided not to go to college. Many people were upset and told me that was an irresponsible choice. Instead of arguing, I learned to ask them questions: Did you go to college? If you went, what did you expect before you went? Did the actual experience meet your expectations? What were the best and the worst parts of it? If you didn't go, why not? What do you feel you missed? What did you do instead? What did you learn from that? Often, this helped me to understand their perspective better, which sometimes meant I could explain my decision in a framework that made sense to them. "So you knew you wanted to be a professor, and the path to that was clearly through college. Good for you for knowing what you wanted and how to get there ... I want to farm and write, and practice and apprenticeship look like better paths to that." Whether or not it offered that kind of common ground, it shifted the tone of the discussion. People were remembering, not lecturing. Their voices and gestures softened. I found that much easier to deal with, and better for the relationship as well.

Ask clarifying questions. "When you say ... do you mean ... ?" "In what circumstances do you believe this is true?" "This is what I think I'm hearing you say. Am I understanding you correctly?" Too often, we hear a few emotionally charged words or phrases from the other person and assume we know what they're thinking. Those assumptions can be very wrong.

I remember one of my own emotionally charged wrong assumptions. Once at a weeklong church retreat, I met someone I liked and admired. We happily talked theology and politics, and then he said, "I'm never going to divorce. It's just wrong."

We'd been walking together. I stopped dead, and then ran after him, glaring. "What do you mean, it's just wrong?" I asked.

"Well, what I said," he said curtly and a bit more loudly. "I figured that much out growing up. No divorce! Marriage is ..."

I wasn't listening. I cut him off. "I know," I said. "I learned that growing up. Marriage is a covenant. Marriage is a sacrament. Marriage is for life. But I learned some other things, too. If he hits you, or if he molests your kids, or if he spends all his time and money on younger women and then comes home and expects you to deal with the debts and diseases, then you need to leave, get a divorce, make sure he doesn't get custody of the kids. If he's done something to warrant it, get a restraining order and file charges, don't just stick around being a submissive Christian wife!"

I realized that I was speaking quite loudly and that he was staring at me.

"But, I ... I'm not crazy! I know nobody would stick around in that kind of marriage," my friend said. "Nobody should. I just meant, no getting a divorce just because you're bored and there's someone more fulfilling out there and never mind the kids."

"Well, of course, you don't get a divorce for that reason!" I said. "I'm not totally without character ..."

At that point we both quieted down and started actually listening. We realized that our position on marriage and divorce was actually about the same, but we were framing it differently. He was thinking of his own frequently remarried parents (whom, by the way, he didn't like to hear dismissed as "totally without character,") of the difficulties their partner-switching caused in his childhood and of his determination not to do as they'd done. I was lucky enough to grow up in a safe home, but I was thinking of some friends I loved who had grown up afraid because their mothers (whom, by the way, I didn't like to hear dismissed as "crazy") had believed that wifely obedience was the first Christian virtue.

I remembered that interaction later in a tense online discussion when someone took me to task for being one of those cruel abortion-rights supporters who don't care about the lives of children. (He had been being lectured by some others about being one of those cruel anti-choice activists who don't care about the rights of women.) I asked if we could step beyond the labels for a moment and think about specific situations. I told him that I believed that life begins before birth, and that the unborn have human rights — but that the women who carried them were also humans with rights. Still, there were some circumstances that had arisen in the lives of people I knew where I couldn't see what was the right choice and I didn't think the government had a right to dictate whose rights were protected. I described a few of those circumstances and asked if he believed that abortion should be illegal in all those cases. He wrote that of course he didn't mean that women who had been raped, or whose lives were in danger, had to continue their pregnancies. What kind of unreasonable person did I think he was? He told his stories of times when he was clear that abortion was wrong. Once again, we were in similar positions, but the language we used to describe those positions was different enough to fuel a quarrel.

Of course, clarifying questions won't always reveal that you're actually on the same page. They may show that you're using the same words to mean different things. (Remember the different meanings of "freedom" and "fairness" discussed in Chapter 1.) Or ... they may show that your basic assumptions and frameworks are poles apart. But at least once you've asked the clarifying questions, there's a better chance that you both know what you're discussing. And ... you've also shown that you're actually paying attention ... treating the other person as though they matter.

A Time to Speak

Once you've listened, you have a better chance of speaking in a way that will allow you and your partner to really converse instead of yelling past each other in the same room. Here are a few rules of thumb which may help to keep the conversation on a constructive track:

Acknowledge what the other person has said.

It's especially important to start with this when the other person is speaking from a place of great pain (like the people I described in Chapter 3 who felt hurt by Christians, or by gay people) or fear (like Grace worrying about her son.) Even in less fraught situations, relationship-building and real dialogue are fostered by starting with some kind of recognition of what the other person has just said. It may help to start with recognition of something that you can identify with. "I hear how proud you are of the hard work you've put in to get where you are now." "I hear how concerned you are about the world your kids are growing up in." "I hear you about how our childhood memories shape our lives."

After doing this, you may be able to speak about your own labors, pride, concerns and memories, while remembering that, however different your party labels are, you're both real people who have things in common. However, Headlee and others urge us not to say, "I know just how you feel, I've experienced that too ..." or speak in a way that seems to be competing with the other person ("I worked harder than you did." "I'm a better parent." "My childhood was healthy, so I'm not a mess like you." "My childhood was harder than yours. What do you have to complain about?")

I once heard two friends, a man and a woman, talking about how they'd each responded to conflict in a community they cared about. He said that as a little boy he'd learned that arguments were unending and unbearable and that conflict was something to avoid at all costs. She listened, nodded and said she heard how hard that must have been. She was briefly quiet, then said that it was odd how different our childhood lessons are and how deeply they shape us. She'd learned as a girl that the intolerable thing was lying; pretending that all is well when in fact something is terribly wrong. She'd learned that directly confronting what's wrong is the only bearable option. They heard each other and cried for each other. They came away with a better understanding of each other — and of themselves.

It may also be helpful and necessary to acknowledge that you've just heard about an experience you can't really imagine having to carry, or a position you can't imagine holding. This shows that you really are listening and not trying to make the other person over in your own image.

Be honest.

If you think it's safe to do so, own your own feelings and the experiences that shape them. "I'm feeling defensive," and "That's really hard for me to hear, because it reminds me of ..." are hard to say, and may be hard to hear, but they form a more honest basis for conversation than an attempt to sound detached and dispassionate when you aren't. They're also more likely to cause the other person to listen carefully and sympathetically — if the other person is at all inclined to be considerate. (If they're not, you may want to consider whether this is someone you really want to converse with.) Don't just give talking points. Tell the stories behind your beliefs. We listen to stories in a different way than to arguments; our sympathy and our imaginations are engaged. Reach out to your listener.

Own your convictions, too. Don't deny what you believe in an attempt to fit in. Acknowledge common ground, but be frank about differences. Pretending and denying tend to make us feel more fearful, resentful and lonely. That's not good for us or for our relationships. Speak your truth.

Admit ignorance. Don't exaggerate or fudge facts to bolster your position; don't say "Everybody knows," when you mean "I think I heard on the radio a while ago ..." It's really not shameful to admit that you don't know everything. "This is what I remember hearing, but I'm not sure my memory is correct," "I'm not sure about that," "I need to think more about that," and "I want to research that and then get back to you," are all honest and constructive statements. They free you from worrying that the other person will be able to poke a hole in your flimsy argument. They also invite the other person to lay down the burden of having to seem to know everything. And, they remind both of you that you're looking for the truth together; not trying to score points off each other.

Be civil.

Even — especially — when the other person's position strikes you as repulsive or untenable. That doesn't mean you can't voice your objection strongly. It does mean you should speak as you'd wish to be spoken to by people who find your position repulsive or untenable. (Trust me, there are people like that out there. Whatever your position is, there are people who can't imagine that any good person could hold it.) Don't resort to name-calling or shaming. As noted in Chapter 4, shaming tends to prompt hostility, shut down open-mindedness and lock both the shamed and the shamer into bunker mode. You can tell the other person why their words or actions dismay you, hurt you or concern you. Don't tell them that only a hateful ignorant animal would say or do what they just said or did. See if you can see some valid reasons for their position. If you can see any, acknowledge them.

Sometimes you won't be able to see anything to validate. Sometimes you really are looking across what seems to be an impassable moral divide. Sometimes you really are appalled by what you see. You can say that, too. But it still matters to speak to the other person as though they're a real human being capable of doing better. Because they are. None of us wants to be judged by the worst thing we ever said or did. Some people, whose worst looks rather appalling, have "hit bottom," seen the harm they did, and spent the rest of their lives trying to heal the damage and preventing other people going down the same wrong road. That's true of people who've committed violent crimes, who've let addictions ruin their lives and hurt the people around them and who've joined cults and hate groups. And so far, none of the stories I've seen suggest that being shamed or screamed at helped to transform their thinking.

It still matters, also, to listen carefully to what people have to say, even when it goes against your deeply held convictions. Those people who leave hate groups do so because they've finally reached the place where they can hear something that challenges their tenaciously held (though misguided) convictions. People can be passionate, sincere and ... wrong! We ourselves can be passionate, sincere and ... wrong! Listening deeply can be one corrective to such wrong convictions.

Try reframing your story in their terms.

This isn't appropriate in all circumstances. Sometimes, there's a fundamental difference of conviction that matters more than the specific issue at hand. But sometimes, if you're trying to get someone to reconsider a particular issue, it helps to frame the issue in terms of their values.

Professors Robb Willer of Stanford and Matthew Feinberg of the University of Toronto conducted several studies showing the effectiveness of moral reframing. They drew on Jonathan Haidt's theories about moral foundations, summarized in Chapter 1, and on related research showing that liberals tended to make moral arguments based on caring for the vulnerable, preventing harm, and treating people fairly (fairness being defined in terms of equality, not merit and deserving.) Conservatives more often made arguments based on patriotism, loyalty, respect for authority, religious sanctity and moral purity. Willer and Feinberg wondered what would happen if liberals were exposed to arguments for typically conservative causes that appealed to liberal values, and vice versa. They prepared two articles in support of same-sex marriage, a typically liberal cause. One article emphasized equal rights (a fairness argument, in the liberal sense.) The other said that "same-sex couples are proud and patriotic Americans" who "contribute to the American economy and society," (a loyalty-based argument.) Self-described conservatives were shown one or the other of the articles before answering questions about same-sex marriage. Those who had just read the article on same-sex couples as proud and patriotic Americans were measurably more supportive of same-sex marriage than those who had read the equal rights argument.

Willer and Feinberg also showed self-described liberals articles supporting increased military spending, a typically conservative cause. One article emphasized pride in our military, which "unifies us both at home and abroad," a loyalty-based message. The other described military service "as a way for the poor and disadvantaged to advance themselves and receive equal standing," a fairness-based message. Then liberals were asked to indicate their support for increased military spending. Those who had read the fairness-based article were more supportive.[72]

I would suggest using this strategy only when you yourself actually share the values to which you're appealing, even if they're not your only or primary values. Otherwise, you may come across as glib or insincere — and may also make it harder for the other person to understand where you're actually coming from. Or, you may misunderstand their framework and just make them angrier. I remember listening to an intense discussion in an international church organization. A liberal U.S. delegate and a conservative Kenyan delegate got into a heated exchange over same-sex marriage. The American said that expanding the narrow traditional definition of marriage would make more room for typically African customs like polygamy. The Kenyan speaker was exceedingly indignant, saying that polygamy was a sin against God. He pointed out that he was not reproaching the U.S. with all its shameful sexual customs, and he expected a similar degree of forbearance from his opponent. Things went downhill from there. Attempting to speak from values you don't share may be almost as dangerous as attempting to speak from a culture you don't share.

But if you and your conversation partner really do hold some values in common, it may serve you well to use these as you explain your position. In Chapter 5, I described how I came to be invited to guest-post liberal articles on a small conservative blog. The first time I accepted this generous invitation I chose to address immigration. I knew the main blogger liked articles with a strong historical tie-in. I had heard some of his like-minded commenters complaining of the excessively emotional and insubstantial speech habits of liberals, and I thought I was writing to suit my audience. I wrote about the anti-Catholic hysteria of the 1800s, in which the "American Party" claimed that the U.S. was being overrun by terrorists who owed their allegiance to a violent and depraved religion and to an alien religious legal code antithetical to the Constitution. I pointed out the parallels with current anti-Muslim narratives. I reminded readers of how deeply and thoroughly Catholics are now woven into the fabric of America. I packed in statistics about the contributions made by, and the very low rate of crimes committed by, Muslims and recent immigrants. I appealed to the readers' sense of fairness, and their concern for vulnerable people fleeing dangerous situations — quintessentially liberal appeals, though I didn't recognize it at the time.

I was surprised at the hostile response I got from blog commenters. Some readers were angry that I had compared Catholics to Muslims, others were angry that I had criticized the good American Protestants of the 1800s who were simply trying to preserve their faith and their country. Others simply told me I was ignorant and un-American and that my preferred policies would imperil our beloved country. Since my host on the blog had a strict civility policy, nobody cursed me out or suggested that I ought to be raped or beheaded, which is sometimes what I hear when I post pro-immigrant remarks online. I was grateful for that, but disheartened at not having made a positive connection.

After waiting several months, and reading several books on cross-partisan dialogue, I wrote another guest post. This one was prompted by reading the host's blog post about how his parents had raised him to honor his elders, his country and his God, and how this led him to feel outraged when people knelt during the national anthem to protest racial injustice, or when people attempted to impose humanitarian limits on the tactics of our military. I thought about that for a while and then wrote about how my mother also had raised me to be considerate of my neighbors, especially the elders, and to try to be a good citizen and a good Christian — and how this had led me to a very different response to racial tensions, protests during the anthem, and military restrictions. My policy conclusions on those issues were as thoroughly opposed to my host's as my policy conclusions on immigration had been. But ... I kept my supporting narrative close to the touchstones I shared with him: Family, faith, community, courtesy, hard work, respect, etc. I was surprised by the complete absence of hostile comments, and the fact that the post was "liked" and even "shared" by a few fairly conservative readers. [73]

Try expanding the frame of the discussion.

While Willer and Feinberg's studies show that speaking to people in their own language can be persuasive, evidence from another source suggests that arguments made with very different language can be persuasive. The Internet forum, Reddit, offered a subforum called "Change My View," a space for people to state their views and invite other people to offer different perspectives and try to change their minds. The original posters were asked to engage with respondents and indicate when or if their minds had been changed. Researchers from Cornell looked at the data after almost two years of discussion on "Change My View." Unsurprisingly, they found that civilly-worded arguments were more likely to be successful, as were long arguments, arguments that cited sources, and arguments that included personal stories. More surprisingly, they found that arguments were more likely to succeed when they used language very different from the language of the original post. The researchers thought this likely meant that the people using new language were also bringing in points of view new to the original poster.[74]

This kind of expansion isn't incompatible with reframing. Consider again, the article in favor of same-sex marriage which conservatives found persuasive. That article appealed to a moral value prized by conservatives (loyalty.) But, it didn't use the language or the value I've most often heard brought up in conservative arguments against same-sex marriage, which often frame it as an offense against purity or against respect for tradition. It put the issue on a new basis — but on a basis that made sense to the intended audience.

Know when to stop.

There's also a fine art to knowing when to stop a conversation. That may need to happen when one of your boundaries has been crossed. This may be a fixed boundary. "As I told you before, I am not willing to talk with you while you're using racial slurs. If you want to talk about this, come back when you're willing to stop doing that." It may also be a matter of your energy running out. "I'm sorry, I want to discuss this with you further, but I have this difficult meeting coming up and I don't have the emotional energy right now. Can we get back to this next week?"

Even without boundary-crossing, a brief exchange can sometimes be more useful than a lengthy one. Analysis of "Change My View" found that up to a certain point, back-and-forth dialogue improved the odds of changing someone's mind, but after that point, further discussion was not helpful. Persuasion was more likely after two exchanges than one, and after three exchanges than two. At four exchanges, the likelihood of persuasion began to fall, and after five exchanges, there was basically no chance of changing someone's mind. I've often been annoyed by people who kept on arguing when I thought we had clearly established a lack of common ground, and I've thought of the definition of a fanatic as "someone who can't change his mind and won't change the subject." Sometimes I have been the fanatic in the room ...

This is measuring back-and-forth in one conversation. There are many stories of people whose views changed after weeks, months or years of interaction with someone whom they saw as different. Persistence of this sort may be helpful, but pounding away at your argument in each encounter will probably do more harm than good.

When things go wrong, acknowledge it. Have compassion for the other person and yourself.

Sometimes you may be able to use these techniques to have deep, moving, cordial, substantive conversations. Sometimes that's not going to work out. Maybe you'll inadvertently hit a sore spot and the other person will blow up. Maybe you'll do the blowing up. Maybe you'll bore or confuse each other, or feel as though you never quite manage to find your way into the same conversation.

Headlee recommends acknowledging openly when things are beginning to go wrong — or, if the problem arises suddenly, acknowledging it after the fact. Say that this conversation didn't turn out as you had hoped. If you know you did something unhelpful, acknowledge it and apologize. Don't wait for the other person to apologize first, even if you think they were being unhelpful too. (This applies in most cases. If the other person has been threatening you and/or dehumanizing you, just get away from them.) If you're not sure what went wrong, ask the other person if there is something they wish you'd handled differently.

Don't put yourself or the other person down just because things didn't work out in the way you'd hoped for. Remember that having civil conversations on contentious topics is really hard work which requires practice as well as goodwill — and perhaps also, a certain amount of good luck. Remember that the work is worth doing, that you're engaged in a process that will help you to see yourself and the other person more clearly and that can help to heal the deep divides in your country and your world.

That doesn't mean it's going to happen smoothly, easily or immediately. During the months of writing this book, I've kept on trying to reach across divides and have civil conversations. I've been frequently frustrated with myself and with other people. I've sometimes felt that the one thing my liberal and conservative friends really share is extreme annoyance with my tendency to say, "Look, those people over there have some valid concerns." Sometimes I think that's because they're stuck in bunker mentality. Sometimes I think it's because I still don't know how to listen deeply enough and speak well enough. But even my failures leave me with some greater ability to empathize with other people who are clearly struggling to be good citizens and good neighbors in this crazy time in this crazy world. When I think I see them failing, I remember my own failures, and remember that at bottom, we're together in this struggle to be honest and kind and to recognize the honesty and kindness in one another. I remind myself of the quote from the Talmud which I have carried with me for years, and have returned to more often in the furor of the past year and a half, "Look ahead. You are not expected to complete the task. Neither are you permitted to lay it down."[75]

One last thing... You now have an opportunity to help others see past their political convictions by simply sharing your opinion on this book with a review on Amazon. This would help me and your fellow readers tremendously.

I also want to give you a chance to win a **$200.00 Amazon Gift Card** as a thank-you for reading this book.

All I ask is that you give me some feedback! You can also copy/paste your *Amazon* or *Goodreads review* and this will also count.

Your opinion is valuable to me. It will only take a minute of your time to let me know what you like and what you didn't like about this book. The hardest part is deciding how to spend the two hundred dollars! Just follow this link.

http://booksfor.review/beyondusandthem

Appendix A

Online Resources:

Different perspectives on political news:
Blue Feed, Red Feed: http://graphics.wsj.com/blue-feed-red-feed/
Trending headlines on assorted topics taken from liberal and conservative Facebook feeds, collected and presented by *The Wall Street Journal* (which takes pains to point out that the content has not been vetted in any way; with this page they're trying to reveal the state of our political dialogue, not to recommend reliable sources for getting accurate information.)

All Sides: www.allsides.com
News articles from left, right, center, and some obscurer positions, sorted by topic. AllSides is more apt to draw from mainstream or reputable news organizations than Blue Feed, Red Feed. AllSides also offers discussion forums and links to other bridge-building organizations.

Resources for Civil Conversations:
The Living Room Conversations Project: https://livingroomconversations.org/
Living Room Conversations bring small groups of liberals and conservatives together for civil dialogues built around questions designed to help people understand each other's experiences and convictions. The LRC site offers guidelines for dialogue, discussion guides for specific topics, news stories from different perspectives, and the chance to sign up for online conversations.

Make Shift Coffee House's resource page: http://makeshiftcoffeehouse.com/want-to-learn-more/ MSCH brings diverse groups of people together for live conversations in Maine. The resource page of their website offers links to manuals on dialogue, bridge-crossing sites and more.

Reddit's "Change My View" forum, discussed in Chapter 7, invites people to post views they're willing to reconsider, read civil responses and indicate whether their minds have changed. Post an opinion, or comment on someone else's, at https://www.reddit.com/r/changemyview/

TED Talks on dialogue and polarization:
Zeynep Tufekci's TED Talk entitled "We're Building a Dystopia Just to Make People Click on Ads," addresses the polarizing power of advertising algorithms and suggests responses: https://www.ted.com/talks/zeynep_tufekci_we_re_building_a_dystopia_just_to_make_people_click_on_ads#t-1332615

Various writers and public figures discussions the need for, and the tools for, dialogue across divides as part of this program: http://www.npr.org/programs/ted-radio-hour/558307433

Books:

Bill Bishop and Robert G. Cushing, *The Big Sort: Why the Clustering of Like-Minded America Is Tearing Us Apart*, **Houghton Mifflin, Boston, 2008**
Describes how Americans are sorting themselves into like-minded political clusters, in their neighborhoods, their faith communities and their social networks—and how this sorting changes and threatens our democracy

Brené Brown, *Braving the Wilderness: The Quest for True Belonging and the Courage to Stand Alone*, **Random House, New York, 2017**
Discusses the psychological dynamics behind our current state of fragmentation and loneliness; distinguishes the precarious sense of belonging that comes with living in a bunker alongside like-minded people from the true sense of belonging that comes from integrity and a clear sense of universal human connection; offers suggestions for accepting our vulnerability and loneliness while building true connections across divides

Jonathan Haidt, *The Righteous Mind: Why Good People Are Divided by Politics and Religion,* **Random House, New York, 2012**
Discusses the differently conceptualized moral foundations of conservatives and liberals, as well as the emotional roots of our convictions and possible ways of disagreeing more constructively with one another

Celeste Headlee, *We Need to Talk: How to Have Conversations That Matter,* **HarperCollins, 2017**
Offers comprehensive suggestions for how to have difficult conversations constructively, based partly on Headlee's career as a radio interviewer

Arlie Russell Hochschild, *Strangers in Their Own Land: Anger and Mourning on the American Right*, **The New Press, New York and London, 2016**
Tells how Hochschild, a liberal author, spent time living among and listening to Tea Party supporters in Louisiana; talks specifically about the deep story and worldview of those people, and generally about how to reach across empathy walls and come to imagine other people's perspectives and experiences.

¹ Pew Research Center, "Partisanship and Political Animosity in 2016," June 22, 2016, http://www.people-press.org/2016/06/22/partisanship-and-political-animosity-in-2016/

² Michael E. Miller, "'Shocking': Neo-Nazis Fly Swastika Flag, Salute at Virginia Shopping Center Where Leader Was Killed," August 26, 2016, *Washington Post*, https://www.washingtonpost.com/news/retropolis/wp/2017/08/25/shocking-neo-nazis-fly-swastika-salute-at-shopping-center-where-leader-was-killed/?utm_term=.251e181dacf3

³ Andrés Miguel Rondón, "In Venezuela We Couldn't Beat Chavez. Don't Make the Same Mistakes We Made," *The Washington Post*, January 27, 2017, https://www.washingtonpost.com/posteverything/wp/2017/01/27/in-venezuela-we-couldnt-stop-chavez-dont-make-the-same-mistakes-we-did/?utm_term=.8c2adf9b2f4d

⁴ Brené Brown, *Braving the Wilderness: The Quest for True Belonging and the Courage to Stand Alone*, Random House, New York, 2017, p. 45
.

⁵ Shel Silverstein, "This Bridge", in *A Light in the Attic*, HarperCollins Publishers, 1981.

⁶ Jonathan Haidt, *The Righteous Mind: Why Good People Are Divided by Politics and Religion*, Random House, New York, 2012, p. 134.

⁷ Peter Brimelow, *Alien Nation: Common Sense About America's Immigration Disaster*, New York, Random House, 1995, p. 249.

[8] For more information on this, see Bill Bishop and Robert G. Cushing, *The Big Sort: Why the Clustering of Like-Minded America Is Tearing Us Apart*, Houghton Mifflin, Boston, 2008, pp 143 ff.

[9] Study described in Bill Bishop and Robert G. Cushing, *The Big Sort: Why the Clustering of Like-Minded America Is Tearing Us Apart*, Houghton Mifflin, Boston, 2008, p. 210.

[10] Tania Lombrozo, "For Some, Scientists Aren't The Authority On Science," November 28, 2016, from the National Public Radio archive at http://www.npr.org/sections/13.7/2016/11/28/503551431/for-some-scientists-aren-t-the-authority-on-science

[11] Joan Dye Gussow, quoted in *Small Wonder* by Barbara Kingsolver, HarperCollins, New York, 2002.

[12] Arlie Russell Hochschild, *Strangers in Their Own Land: Anger and Mourning on the American Right*, The New Press, New York and London, 2016, page 71.

[13] Arlie Russell Hochschild, *Strangers in Their Own Land: Anger and Mourning on the American Right*, The New Press, New York and London, 2016, page 185.

[14] Norman Vincent Peale in *The Power of Positive Thinking*, quoted in Michael Kruse, "The Power of Trump's Positive Thinking," *Politico*, October 13, 2017, http://www.politico.com/magazine/story/2017/10/13/donald-trump-positive-thinking-215704

[15] Quoted in Michael Kruse, "The Power of Trump's Positive Thinking," *Politico*, October 13, 2017, http://www.politico.com/magazine/story/2017/10/13/donald-trump-positive-thinking-215704

[16] Arlie Russell Hochschild, *Strangers in Their Own Land: Anger and Mourning on the American Right*, The New Press, New York and London, 2016, pp 217-218.

[17] Bobby Azarian, "Fear and Anxiety Drive Conservatives' Political Attitudes," Psychology Today, December 31, 2016, https://www.psychologytoday.com/blog/mind-in-the-machine/201612/fear-and-anxiety-drive-conservatives-political-attitudes

[18] Vinita Mehta, "Why Liberals And Conservatives Think So Differently," Psychology Today, February 27, 2017, https://www.psychologytoday.com/blog/head-games/201702/why-liberals-and-conservatives-think-so-differently

[19] Sean Wocjik, quoted in Mandy Oaklander, "Liberals Are More Honest Than Conservatives When They Smile," *Time Health*, Mar 13, 2015, http://time.com/3744433/liberals-conservatives-happiness/

[20] Lisa Bortolotti and Magdalena Antrobus, "Costs and benefits of realism and optimism," Current Opinion in Psychiatry, 2015 Mar, 28 (2): 194-198, https://www.ncbi.nlm.nih.gov/pmc/articles/PMC4323577/

[21] Arlie Russell Hochschild, *Strangers in Their Own Land: Anger and Mourning on the American Right*, The New Press, New York and London, 2016, page 189.

22 Arlie Russell Hochschild, *Strangers in Their Own Land: Anger and Mourning on the American Right*, The New Press, New York and London, 2016, page 179.

23 Arlie Russell Hochschild, *Strangers in Their Own Land: Anger and Mourning on the American Right*, The New Press, New York and London, 2016, page 124.

24 Elizabeth Weise, "Russian fake accounts showed posts to 126 million Facebook users," USA Today, Oct. 30, 2017, https://www.usatoday.com/story/tech/2017/10/30/russian-fake-accounts-showed-posts-126-million-facebook-users/815342001/

25 Adam Entous, Craig Timberg and Elizabeth Dwoskin, "Russian operatives used Facebook ads to exploit division over Black Lives Matter, Muslims," The Washington Post, September 25, 2017, https://www.washingtonpost.com/business/technology/russian-operatives-used-facebook-ads-to-exploit-divisions-over-black-political-activism-and-muslims/2017/09/25/4a011242-a21b-11e7-ade1-76d061d56efa_story.html

26 https://freedomdaily.com/pro-baseball-stadium-lockdown-thousands-screaming-muslims-swarm-field-sick-reason/

27 Described by Elizabeth Kolbert in "Why the Facts Don't Change Our Minds," *The New Yorker,* February 27, 2017, https://www.newyorker.com/magazine/2017/02/27/why-facts-dont-change-our-minds

28 Described by Elizabeth Kolbert in "Why the Facts Don't Change Our Minds," *The New Yorker,* February 27, 2017, https://www.newyorker.com/magazine/2017/02/27/why-facts-dont-change-our-minds

29 Quoted in Bill Bishop, *The Big Sort: Why the Clustering of Like-Minded America Is Tearing Us Apart*, Houghton Mifflin, New York, 2008, p. 285.

30 For more information see Zeynep Tufekci's TED Talk entitled "We're building a dystopia just to make people click on ads," *TED Global*, September 2017, https://www.ted.com/talks/zeynep_tufekci_we_re_building_a_dystopia_just_to_make_people_click_on_ads#t-1332615

31 Bill Bishop, *The Big Sort: Why the Clustering of Like-Minded America Is Tearing Us Apart*, Houghton Mifflin, New York, 2008, p. 39.

32 Bill Bishop, *The Big Sort: Why the Clustering of Like-Minded America Is Tearing Us Apart*, Houghton Mifflin, New York, 2008, p. 6.

33 Hannah Arendt, *The Origins of Totalitarianism*, 1951, Chapter 2 page 80 and Chapter 13 subsection 3.

34 Harry Frankfurt, quoted in Brené Brown's *Braving the Wilderness: The Quest for True Belonging and the Courage to Stand Alone*, Random House, New York, 2017, p. 89.

35 Brené Brown, *Braving the Wilderness: The Quest for True Belonging and the Courage to Stand Alone*, Random House, New York, 2017, p.93.

36 Described in Bret Stetka, "Why Everyone Should Read Harry Potter," Scientific American, September 9, 2014, https://www.scientificamerican.com/article/why-everyone-should-read-harry-potter/

³⁷ David Niewert, "When white nationalists chant their weird slogans, what do they mean?", Southern Poverty Law Center, October 10, 2017, https://www.splcenter.org/hatewatch/2017/10/10/when-white-nationalists-chant-their-weird-slogans-what-do-they-mean

³⁸ Kenneth Dowler, "Media Consumption and Public Attitudes Toward Crime and Justice," Journal of Criminal Justice and Popular Culture, 10(2) (2003), pp 109-126, http://www.albany.edu/scj/jcjpc/vol10is2/dowler.html

³⁹ Jonathan Haidt, *The Righteous Mind: Why Good People Are Divided by Politics and Religion,* Random House, New York, 2012, p. 81.

⁴⁰ Story told more fully in "A 'Recovering Skinhead' On Leaving Racism Behind," interview between Dave Davies and Frank Meeink on Fresh Air, NPR.org transcript at http://www.npr.org/templates/transcript/transcript.php?storyId=125514655, and in *Autobiography of a Recovering Skinhead* by Frank Meeink and Jody Roy, Hawthorne Books, 2009.

⁴¹ Brené Brown, *Braving the Wilderness: The Quest for True Belonging and the Courage to Stand Alone,* Random House, New York, 2017, p.14.

⁴² Arlie Russell Hochschild, *Strangers in Their Own Land: Anger and Mourning on the American Right,* The New Press, New York and London, 2016, p. 71.

⁴³ Arlie Russell Hochschild, *Strangers in Their Own Land: Anger and Mourning on the American Right,* The New Press, New York and London, 2016, p. 52.

44 Arlie Russell Hochschild, *Strangers in Their Own Land: Anger and Mourning on the American Right*, The New Press, New York and London, 2016, pp 176-177.

45 Tony McAleer quoted in Jason Byassee's "Confessions of a Former White Supremacist," *Sojourners*, August 2017, https://sojo.net/magazine/august-2017/confessions-former-white-supremacist

46 Jonathan Haidt, *The Righteous Mind: Why Good People Are Divided by Politics and Religion*, Random House, New York, 2012, p. xxii.

47 Brené Brown, *Braving the Wilderness: The Quest for True Belonging and the Courage to Stand Alone*, Random House, New York, 2017, p. 55.

48 Brené Brown, *Braving the Wilderness: The Quest for True Belonging and the Courage to Stand Alone*, Random House, New York, 2017, p. 54.

49 Jonathan Haidt, *The Righteous Mind: Why Good People Are Divided by Politics and Religion*, Random House, New York, 2012, p. 284.

50 **Paraic O'Brien, "Exclusive: Neo-Nazi and National Front Organiser Quits Movement, Opens up About Jewish Heritage, Comes Out as Gay," *Channel 4 News, UK*, October 17, 2017,** https://www.channel4.com/news/neo-nazi-national-front-organiser-quits-movement-comes-out-as-gay-kevin-wilshaw-jewish-heritage

51 Bill Bishop, *The Big Sort: Why the Clustering of Like-Minded America Is Tearing Us Apart*, Houghton Mifflin, New York, 2008, p. 77.

52 Bill Bishop, *The Big Sort: Why the Clustering of Like-Minded America Is Tearing Us Apart*, Houghton Mifflin, New York, 2008, p. 248.

53 Robert D. Putnam and David E. Campbell, *American Grace: How Religion Unites and Divides Us,* Simon & Schuster, New York, 2010, p. 394.

54 Bill Bishop, *The Big Sort: Why the Clustering of Like-Minded America Is Tearing Us Apart*, Houghton Mifflin, New York, 2008, pp 242-243.

55 Brené Brown, *Braving the Wilderness: The Quest for True Belonging and the Courage to Stand Alone*, Random House, New York, 2017, pp 100-101.

56 Arlie Russell Hochschild, *Strangers in Their Own Land: Anger and Mourning on the American Right*, The New Press, New York and London, 2016, p. 135.

57 Arlie Russell Hochschild, *Strangers in Their Own Land: Anger and Mourning on the American Right*, The New Press, New York and London, 2016, p. 23.

58 Bill Bishop and Robert G. Cushing, *The Big Sort: Why the Clustering of Like-Minded America Is Tearing Us Apart*, Houghton Mifflin, Boston, 2008, p. 69.

59 Brené Brown, *Braving the Wilderness: The Quest for True Belonging and the Courage to Stand Alone*, Random House, New York, 2017, pp 50-51.

60 Brené Brown, *Braving the Wilderness: The Quest for True Belonging and the Courage to Stand Alone*, Random House, New York, 2017, p. 45.

61 Bill Moyers, "A Conversation with Maya Angelou," November 21, 1973, http://billmoyers.com/content/conversation-maya-angelou/

62 Brené Brown, *Braving the Wilderness: The Quest for True Belonging and the Courage to Stand Alone*, Random House, New York, 2017, p. 32.

63 Quoted by Brené Brown in *Braving the Wilderness: The Quest for True Belonging and the Courage to Stand Alone*, Random House, New York, 2017, p. 147.

64 Quoted by Brené Brown in *Braving the Wilderness: The Quest for True Belonging and the Courage to Stand Alone*, Random House, New York, 2017, p. 147.

65 Wendell Berry, *That Distant Land: The Collected Stories*, Shoemaker & Hoard, Washington DC, p. 356.

66 Judith Shulevitz, "In College and Hiding from Scary Ideas," New York Times, March 21, 2015, https://www.nytimes.com/2015/03/22/opinion/sunday/judith-shulevitz-hiding-from-scary-ideas.html

67 "How One Man Convinced 200 Ku Klux Klan Members to Give Up Their Robes," interview between Dwane Brown and Daryl Davis, NPR, August 20, 2017, http://www.npr.org/templates/transcript/transcript.php?storyId=544861933

68 Maria Saporta, "Civil rights icon Xernona Clayton's unlikely friendship with a KKK Grand Dragon," May 1, 2007, http://www.atlantamagazine.com/civilrights/xernona-clayton-kkk-grand-dragon-calvin-craig/

69 Arlie Russell Hochschild, *Strangers in Their Own Land: Anger and Mourning on the American Right*, The New Press, New York and London, 2016, p 4.

70 Brené Brown, *Braving the Wilderness: The Quest for True Belonging and the Courage to Stand Alone*, Random House, New York, 2017, p. 131.

71 Interview between Celeste Headlee and Guy Raz, "Dialogue and Exchange," *TED Radio Hour,* October 27, 2017, http://www.npr.org/2017/10/17/560195583/celeste-headlee-how-can-we-have-civil-conversations-with-the-other-side

72 Rob Willer and Matthew Feinberg, "The Key to Political Persuasion," The New York Times, November 23, 2015, https://www.nytimes.com/2015/11/15/opinion/sunday/the-key-to-political-persuasion.html

73 Joanna Hoyt, "The Ties that Divide, part 2: Christianity and Citizenship," Plain Speaking History, October 15, 2017, http://www.plainspeakinghistory.com/the-ties-that-divide-part-2-christianity-and-citizenship/

74 Ana Swanson, "How to change someone's mind according to science," Washington Post, February 10, 2016, https://www.washingtonpost.com/news/wonk/wp/2016/02/10/how-to-change-someones-mind-according-to-science/?utm_term=.6e827fbe4c53

75 *Pirkei Avot* 2:20-21.

9 781976 970184